IS THIS ANOTHER COMPLAINT, BEETLE BAILEY?

Here's another in the happy series of books based on one of the most famous comic strips in the country. Once again the madcap inmates of Camp Swampy valiantly strive to overcome their own ineptitude—and succeed in delighting us on every page.

Mort Walker again gives us a barrel of laughs in his marvelous cartoons concerning the most unprofessional soldier in the army!

Beetle Bailey Books from Tempo

ABOUT FACE, BEETLE BAILEY
BEETLE BAILEY
BEETLE BAILEY: AT EASE
BEETLE BAILEY: FALL OUT LAUGHING
BEETLE BAILEY: GIVE US A SMILE
BEETLE BAILEY: I DON'T WANT TO BE HERE ANY MORE THAN YOU DO
BEETLE BAILEY: I'LL FLIP YOU FOR IT
BEETLE BAILEY: I'LL THROW THE BOOK AT YOU
BEETLE BAILEY: IS THAT ALL?
BEETLE BAILEY: I THOUGHT YOU HAD THE COMPASS
BEETLE BAILEY: ON PARADE
BEETLE BAILEY: SHAPE UP OR SHIP OUT
BEETLE BAILEY: WHAT IS IT NOW?
DON'T MAKE ME LAUGH, BEETLE BAILEY
I JUST WANT TO TALK TO YOU, BEETLE BAILEY
IS THIS ANOTHER COMPLAINT, BEETLE BAILEY?
OTTO
PEACE, BEETLE BAILEY
TAKE A WALK, BEETLE BAILEY
TAKE TEN, BEETLE BAILEY
YOU'RE OUT OF HUP, BEETLE BAILEY
WHO'S IN CHARGE HERE, BEETLE BAILEY?

Is This Another Complaint, beetle bailey?

Mort Walker

TEMPO BOOKS, NEW YORK

IS THIS ANOTHER COMPLAINT, BEETLE BAILEY?

A Tempo Book/published by arrangement with
King Features Syndicate, Inc.

PRINTING HISTORY
Tempo edition / March 1983

All rights reserved.
Copyright © 1980, 1981, 1983 by King Features Syndicate, Inc.
This book may not be reproduced in whole
or in part, by mimeograph or any other means,
without permission. For information address: Tempo Books,
200 Madison Avenue, New York, N.Y. 10016

ISBN: 0-448-13777-1

Tempo Books are published by Charter Communications, Inc.
200 Madison Avenue, New York, New York 10016.
Tempo Books are registered in the United States Patent Office.
PRINTED IN THE UNITED STATES OF AMERICA

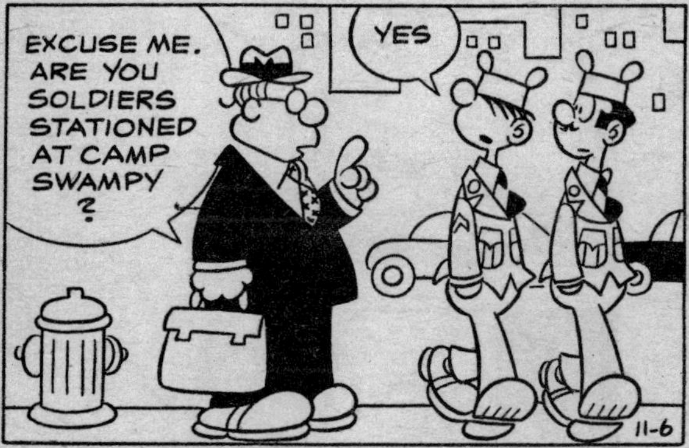
EXCUSE ME. ARE YOU SOLDIERS STATIONED AT CAMP SWAMPY?
YES
11-6

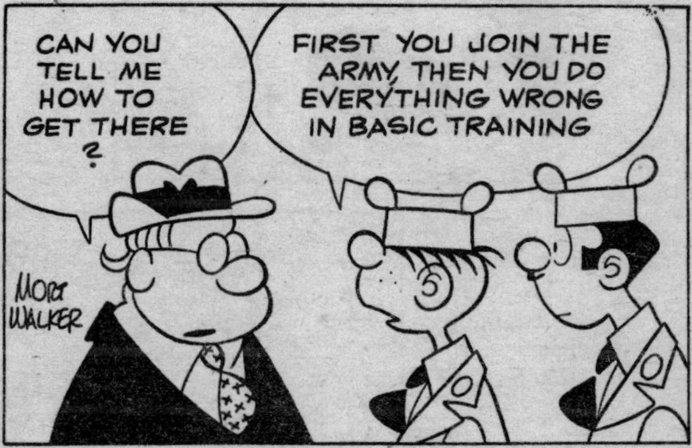
CAN YOU TELL ME HOW TO GET THERE?
FIRST YOU JOIN THE ARMY, THEN YOU DO EVERYTHING WRONG IN BASIC TRAINING
MORT WALKER

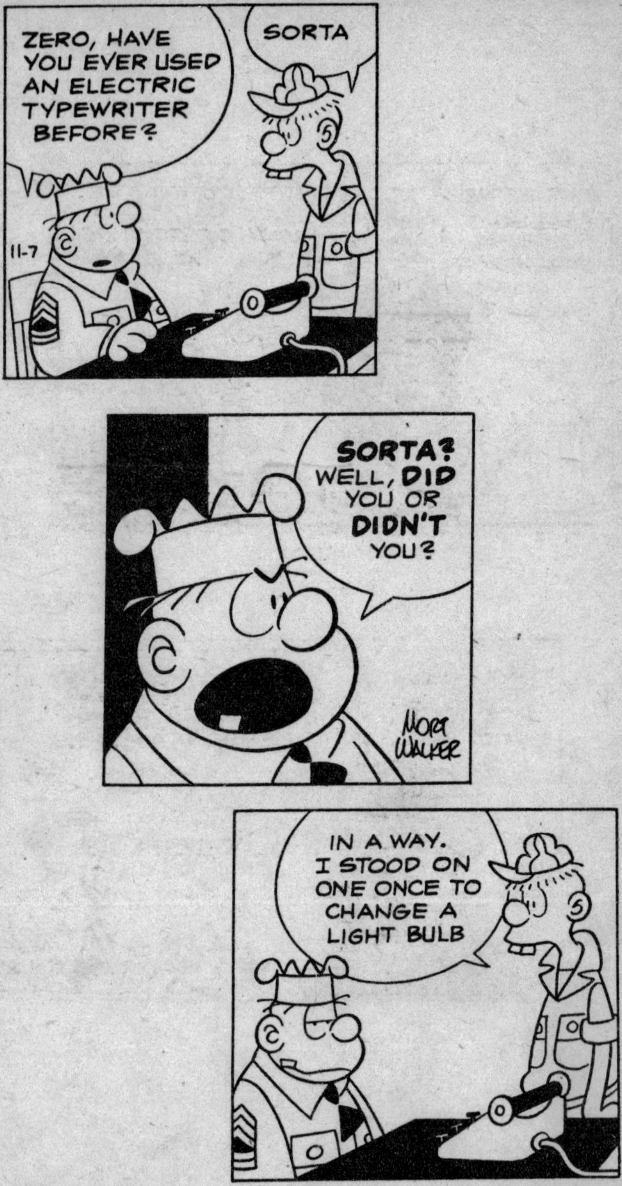
ZERO, HAVE YOU EVER USED AN ELECTRIC TYPEWRITER BEFORE?
SORTA
11-7
SORTA? WELL, DID YOU OR DIDN'T YOU?
MORT WALKER
IN A WAY. I STOOD ON ONE ONCE TO CHANGE A LIGHT BULB

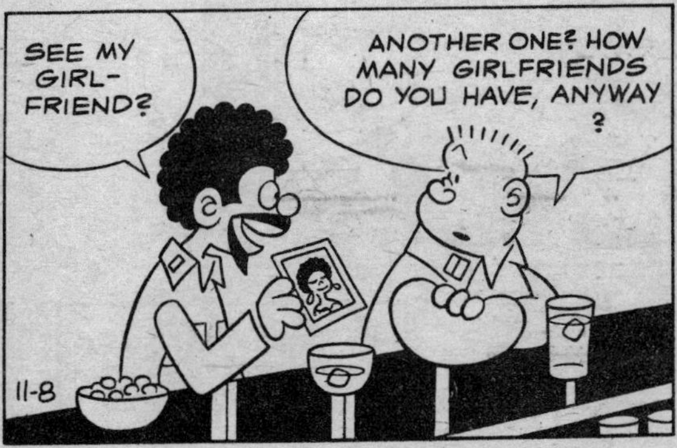
SEE MY GIRL-FRIEND?
ANOTHER ONE? HOW MANY GIRLFRIENDS DO YOU HAVE, ANYWAY?
11-8

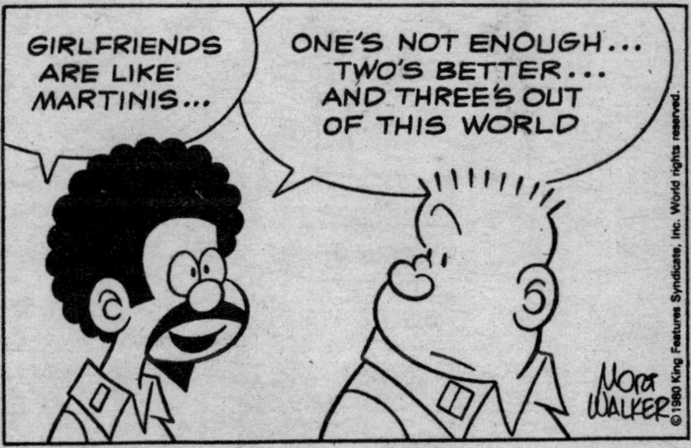
GIRLFRIENDS ARE LIKE MARTINIS...
ONE'S NOT ENOUGH... TWO'S BETTER... AND THREE'S OUT OF THIS WORLD
MORT WALKER
© 1980 King Features Syndicate, Inc. World rights reserved.

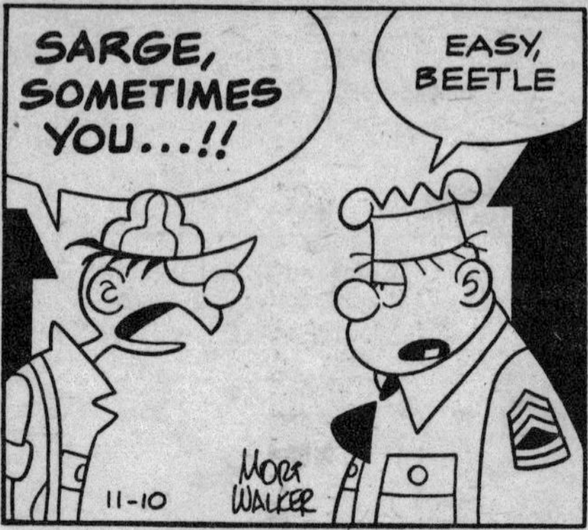
SARGE, SOMETIMES YOU...!!
EASY, BEETLE
11-10
MORT WALKER

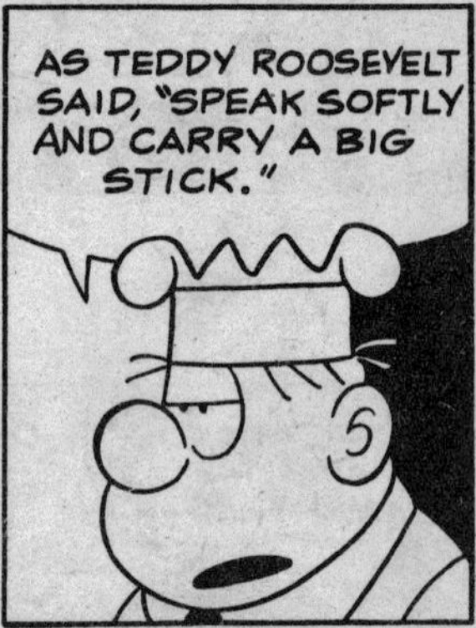
AS TEDDY ROOSEVELT SAID, "SPEAK SOFTLY AND CARRY A BIG STICK."

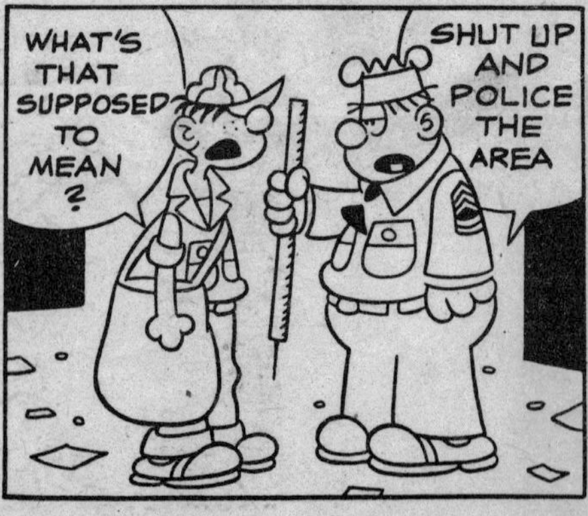
WHAT'S THAT SUPPOSED TO MEAN ?
SHUT UP AND POLICE THE AREA

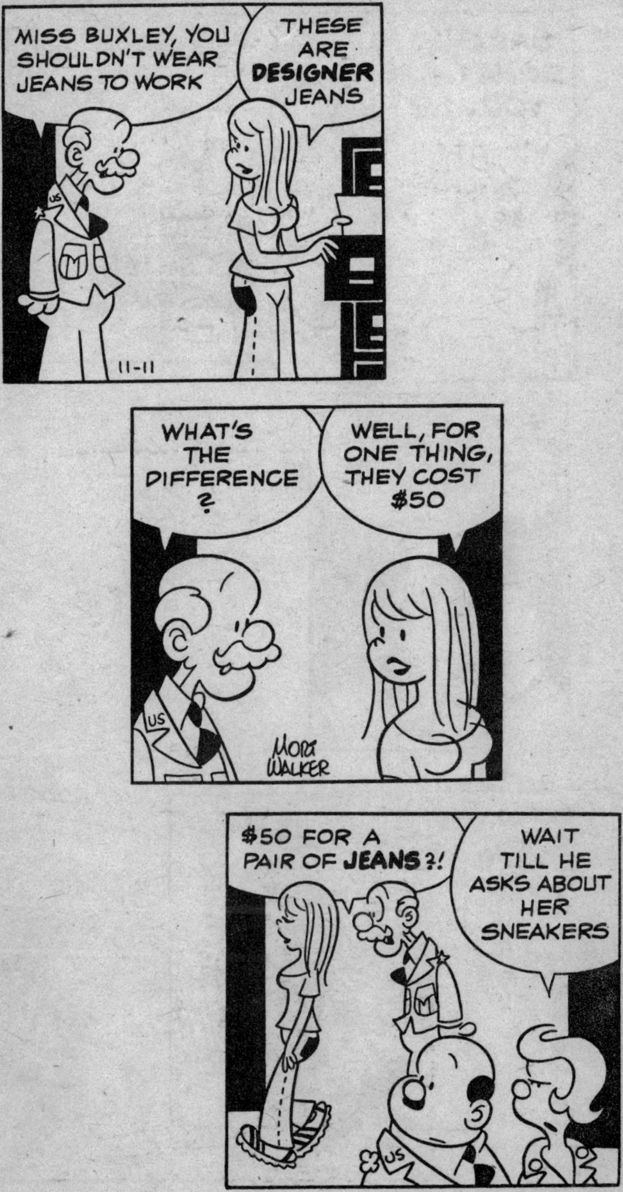
MISS BUXLEY, YOU SHOULDN'T WEAR JEANS TO WORK
THESE ARE **DESIGNER** JEANS
11-11
WHAT'S THE DIFFERENCE ?
WELL, FOR ONE THING, THEY COST $50
MORT WALKER
$50 FOR A PAIR OF **JEANS** ?!
WAIT TILL HE ASKS ABOUT HER SNEAKERS

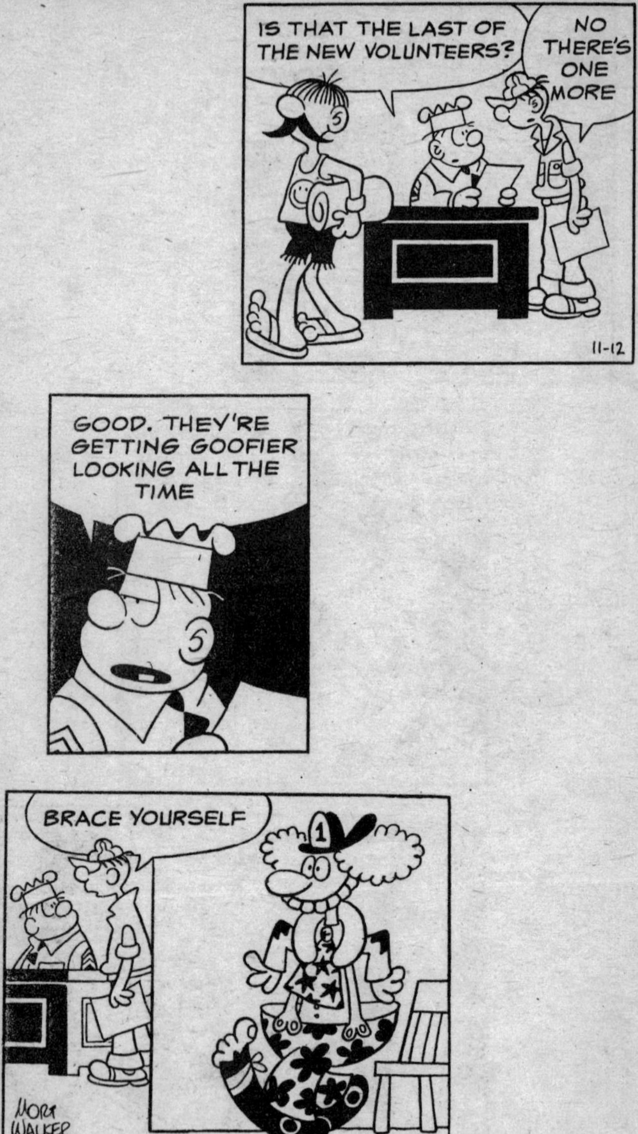
IS THAT THE LAST OF THE NEW VOLUNTEERS?
NO THERE'S ONE MORE
11-12
GOOD. THEY'RE GETTING GOOFIER LOOKING ALL THE TIME
BRACE YOURSELF
MORT WALKER

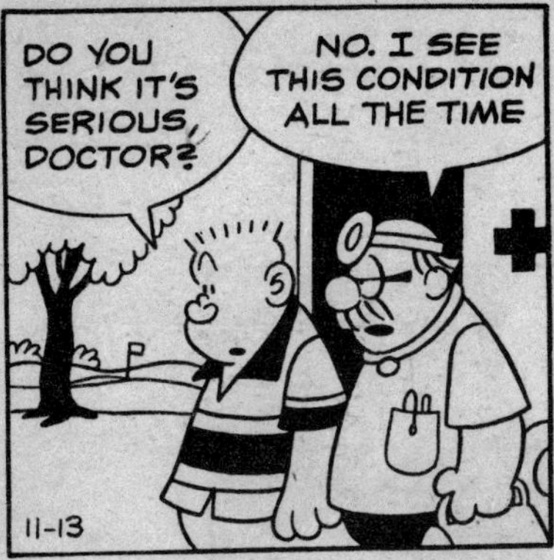
DO YOU THINK IT'S SERIOUS, DOCTOR?
NO. I SEE THIS CONDITION ALL THE TIME
11-13

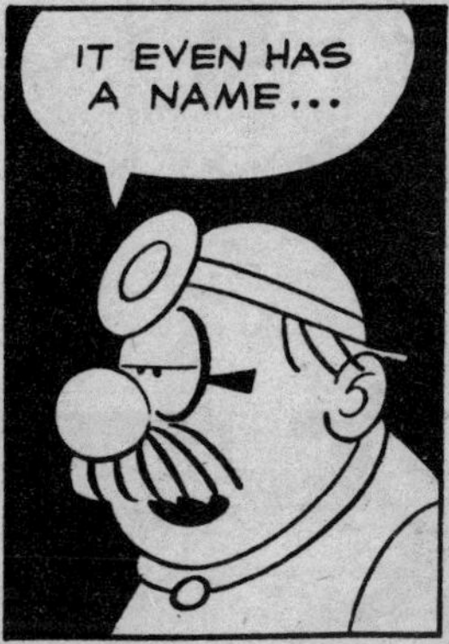
IT EVEN HAS A NAME...

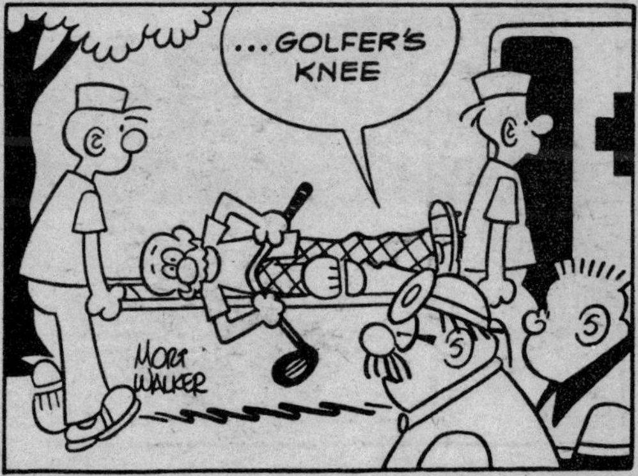
...GOLFER'S KNEE
MORT WALKER

NOW YOU'VE DONE IT, BEETLE! YOU'VE ROLLED THE TANK OVER ON ITS SIDE!
SORRY, SARGE. BETTER CLIMB OUT AND SEE IF THERE'S ANY DAMAGE
SARGE?
MORT WALKER
11-14

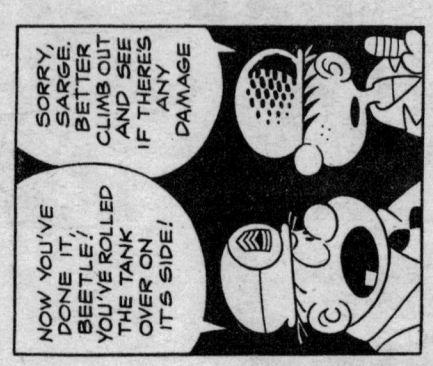

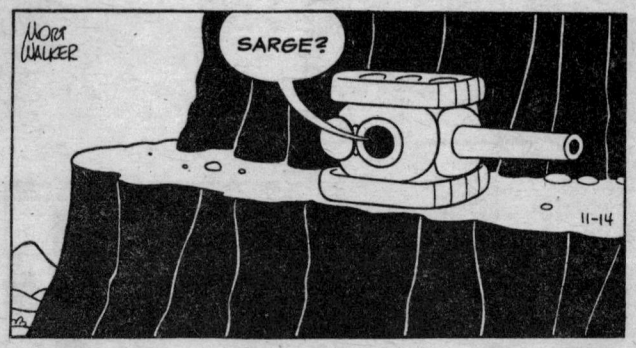

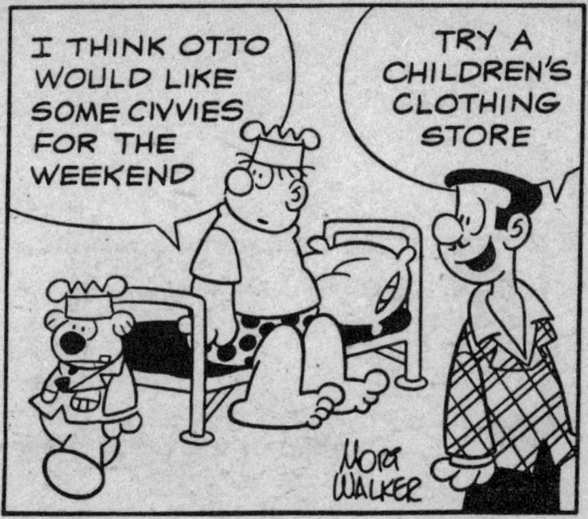
I THINK OTTO WOULD LIKE SOME CIVVIES FOR THE WEEKEND
TRY A CHILDREN'S CLOTHING STORE
MORT WALKER

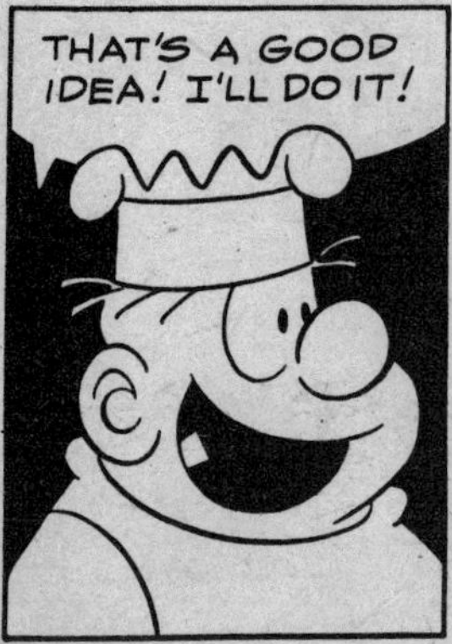
THAT'S A GOOD IDEA! I'LL DO IT!

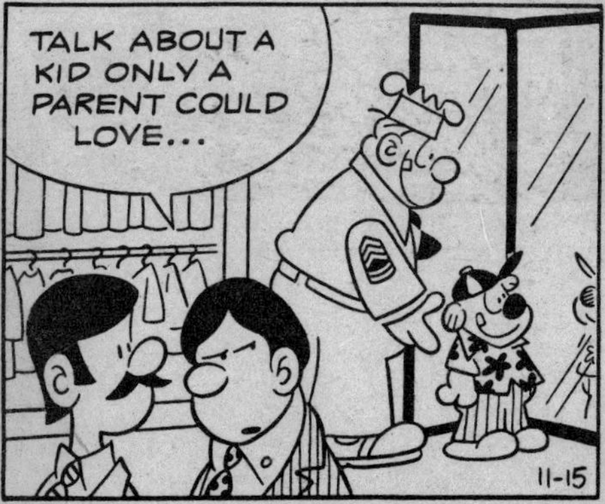
TALK ABOUT A KID ONLY A PARENT COULD LOVE...
11-15

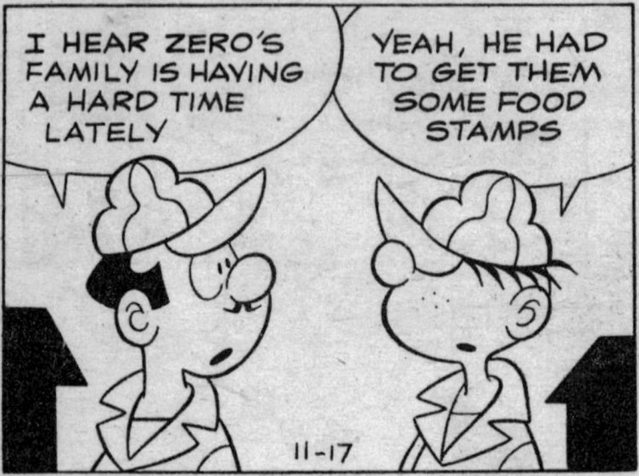
I HEAR ZERO'S FAMILY IS HAVING A HARD TIME LATELY
YEAH, HE HAD TO GET THEM SOME FOOD STAMPS
11-17

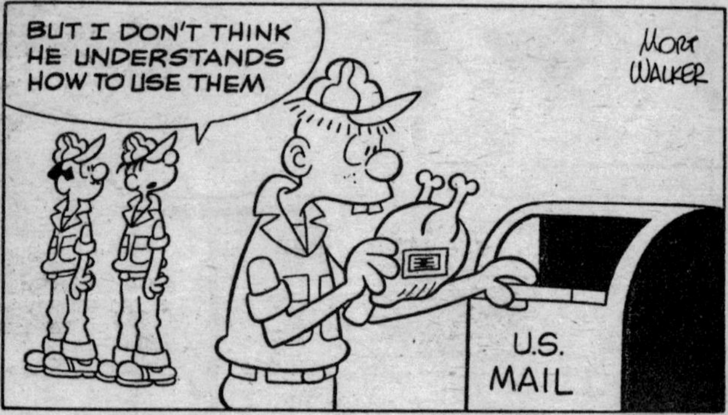
BUT I DON'T THINK HE UNDERSTANDS HOW TO USE THEM
MORT WALKER
U.S. MAIL

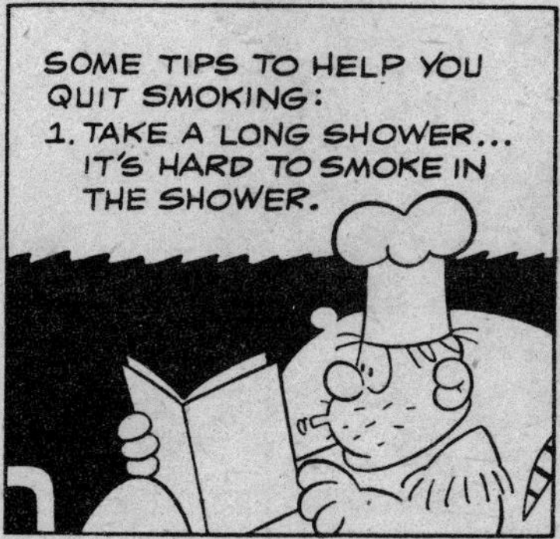
SOME TIPS TO HELP YOU QUIT SMOKING:
1. TAKE A LONG SHOWER... IT'S HARD TO SMOKE IN THE SHOWER.

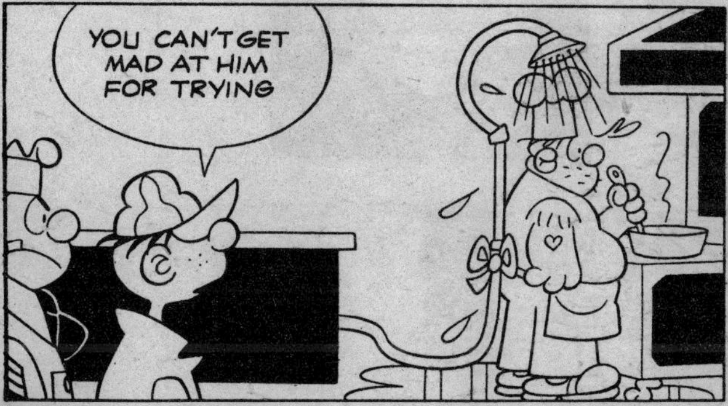
YOU CAN'T GET MAD AT HIM FOR TRYING

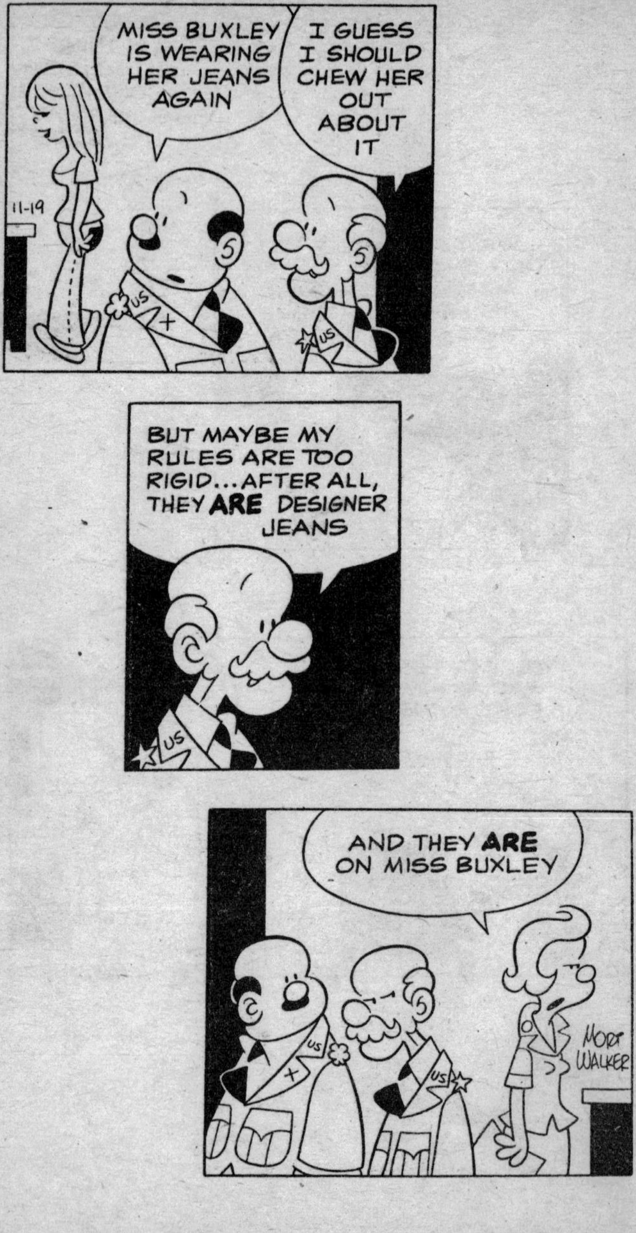
11-19
MISS BUXLEY IS WEARING HER JEANS AGAIN
I GUESS I SHOULD CHEW HER OUT ABOUT IT
BUT MAYBE MY RULES ARE TOO RIGID...AFTER ALL, THEY **ARE** DESIGNER JEANS
AND THEY **ARE** ON MISS BUXLEY
MORT WALKER

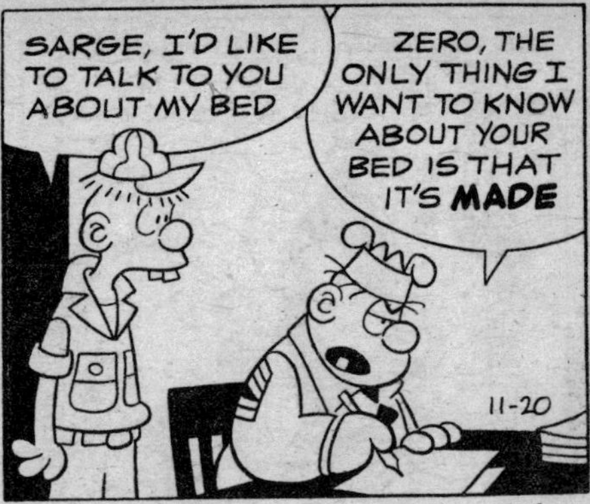
SARGE, I'D LIKE TO TALK TO YOU ABOUT MY BED
ZERO, THE ONLY THING I WANT TO KNOW ABOUT YOUR BED IS THAT IT'S **MADE**
11-20

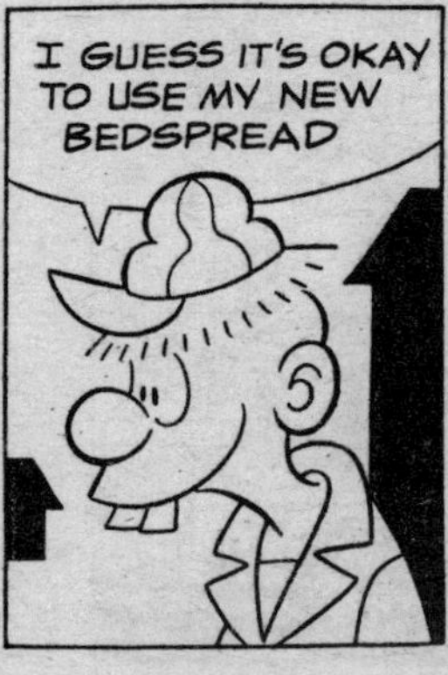
I GUESS IT'S OKAY TO USE MY NEW BEDSPREAD

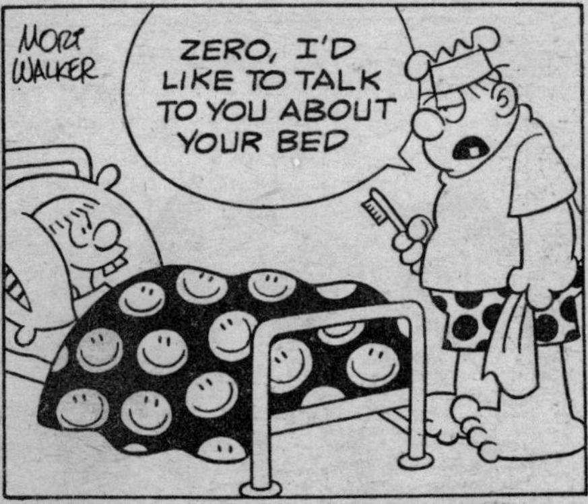
MORT WALKER
ZERO, I'D LIKE TO TALK TO YOU ABOUT YOUR BED

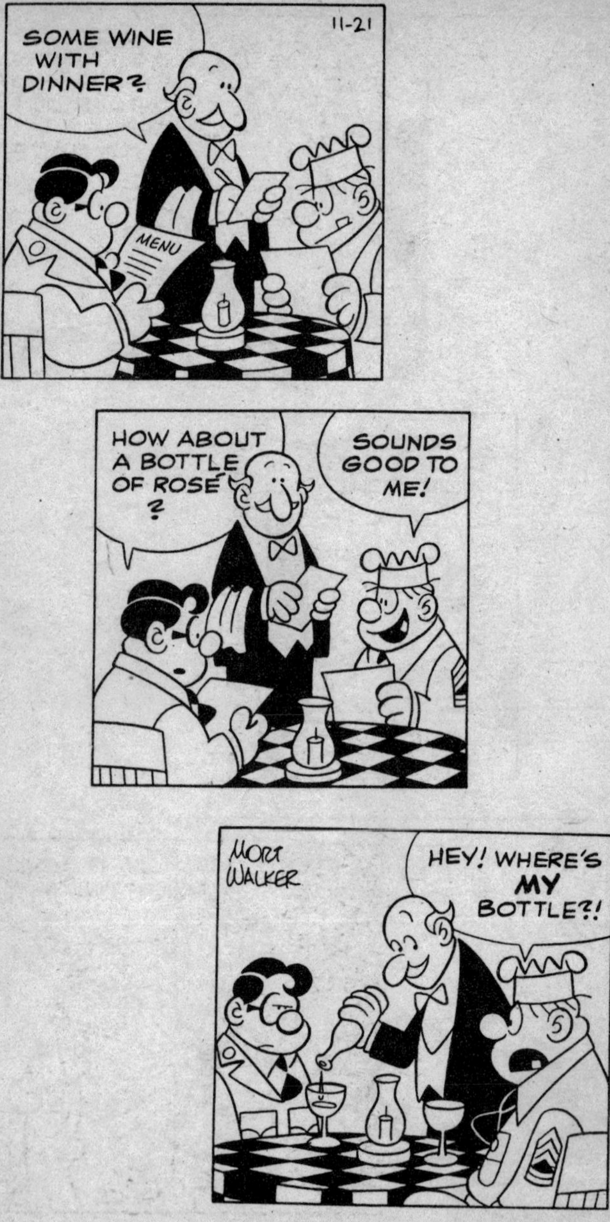
11-21
SOME WINE WITH DINNER?
MENU
HOW ABOUT A BOTTLE OF ROSÉ?
SOUNDS GOOD TO ME!
MORT WALKER
HEY! WHERE'S MY BOTTLE?!

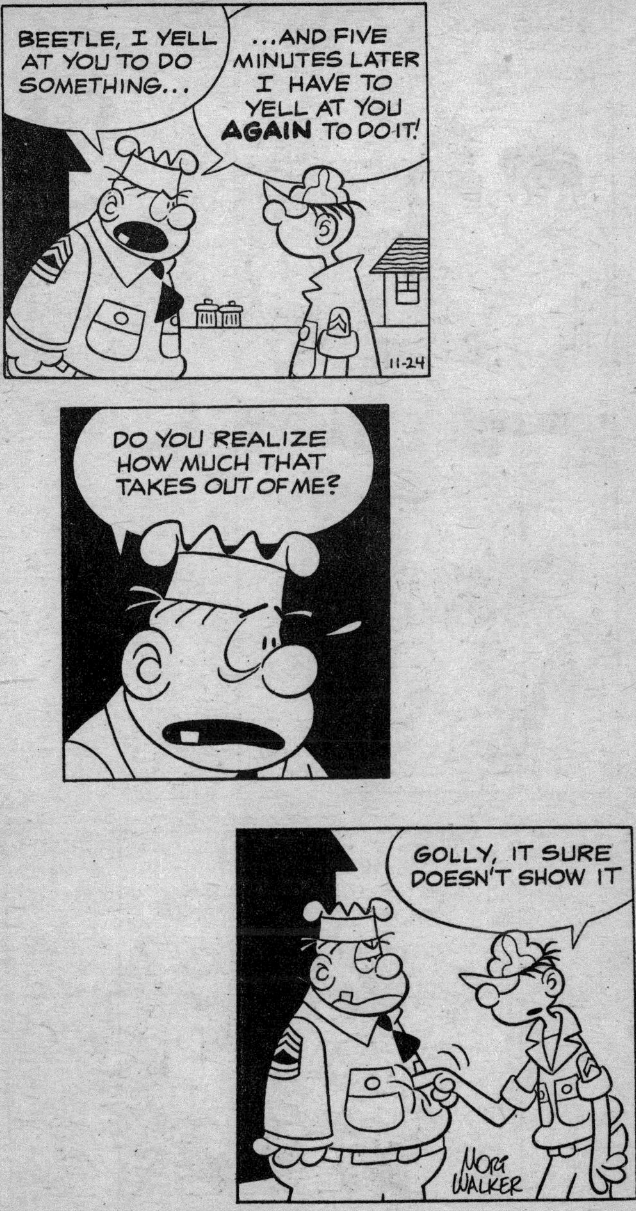
BEETLE, I YELL AT YOU TO DO SOMETHING...
...AND FIVE MINUTES LATER I HAVE TO YELL AT YOU AGAIN TO DO IT!
11-24
DO YOU REALIZE HOW MUCH THAT TAKES OUT OF ME?
GOLLY, IT SURE DOESN'T SHOW IT
MORT WALKER

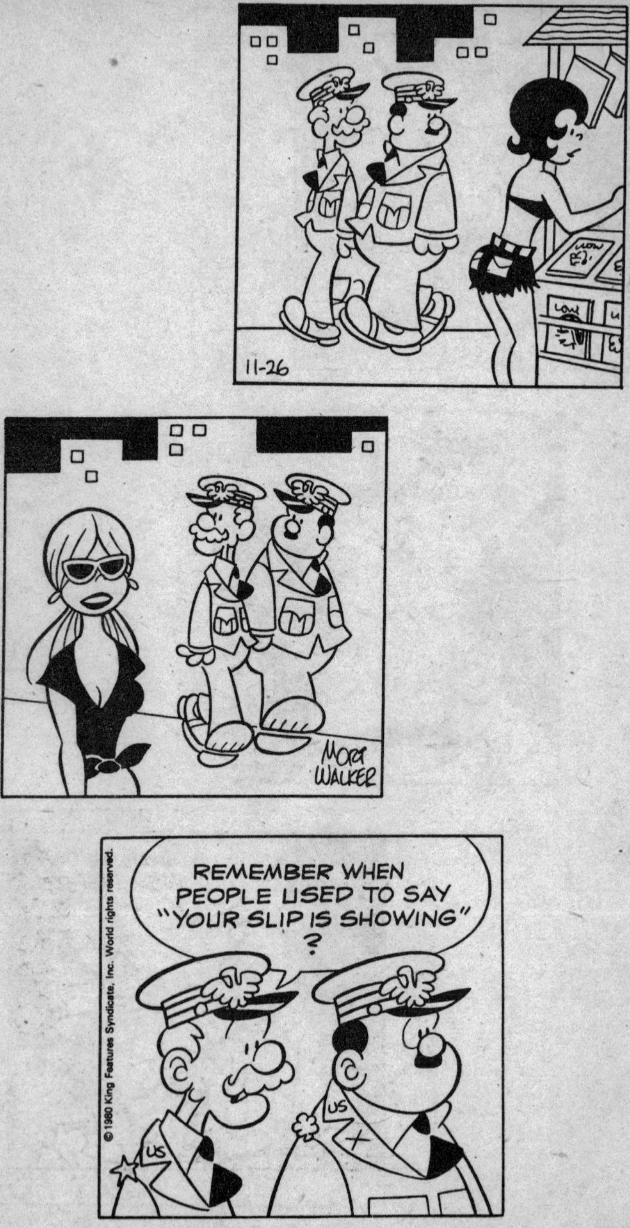
11-26
MORT WALKER
REMEMBER WHEN PEOPLE USED TO SAY "YOUR SLIP IS SHOWING"?
US
US

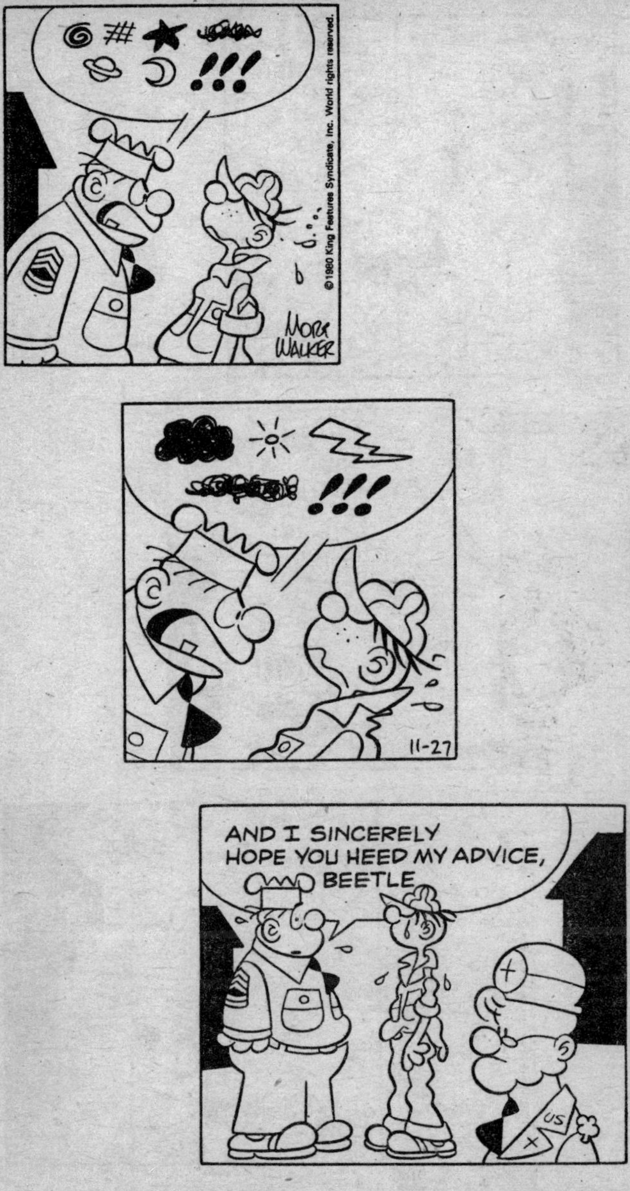
©1980 King Features Syndicate, Inc. World rights reserved.
MORT WALKER
11-27
AND I SINCERELY HOPE YOU HEED MY ADVICE, BEETLE
US

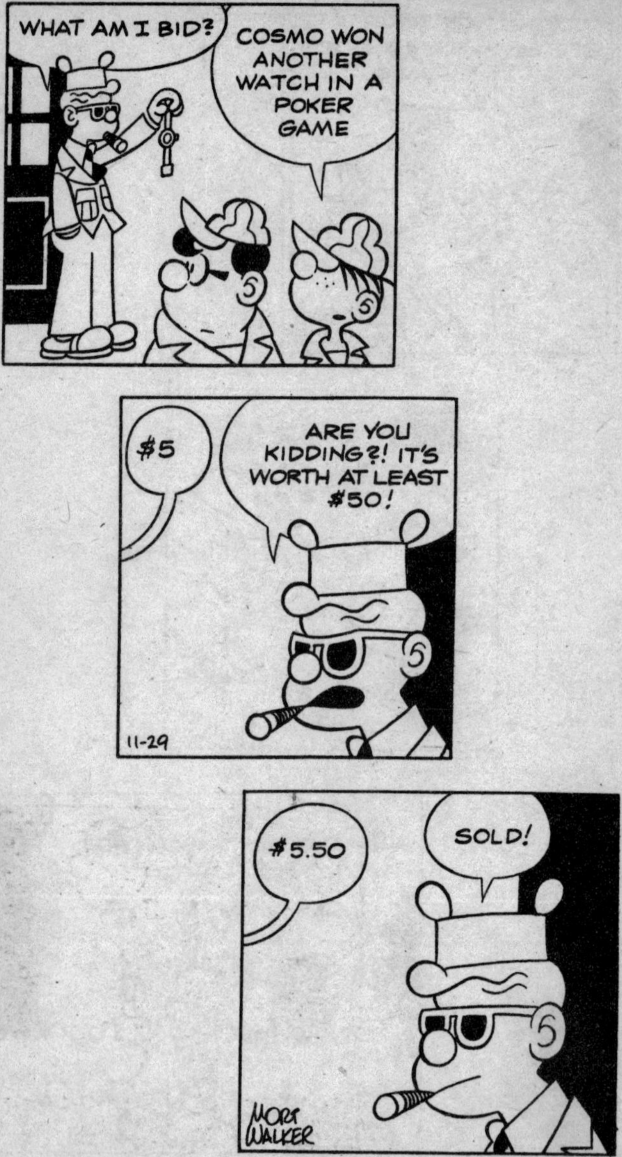
WHAT AM I BID?
COSMO WON ANOTHER WATCH IN A POKER GAME
$5
ARE YOU KIDDING?! IT'S WORTH AT LEAST $50!
11-29
$5.50
SOLD!
MORT WALKER

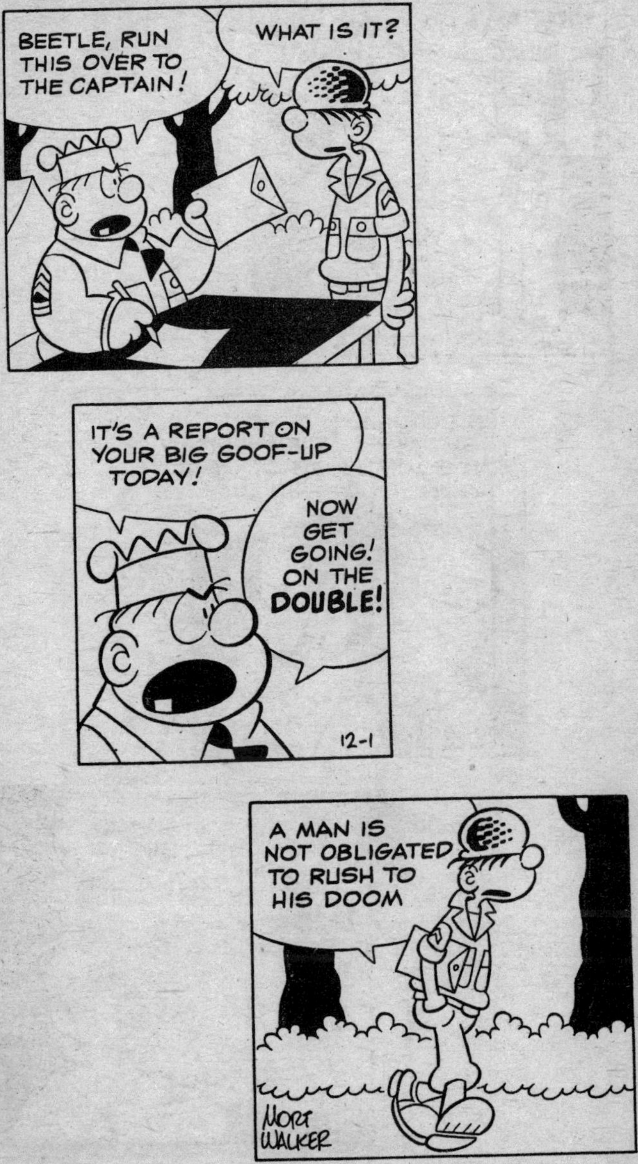
BEETLE, RUN THIS OVER TO THE CAPTAIN!
WHAT IS IT?
IT'S A REPORT ON YOUR BIG GOOF-UP TODAY!
NOW GET GOING! ON THE **DOUBLE!**
12-1
A MAN IS NOT OBLIGATED TO RUSH TO HIS DOOM
MORT WALKER

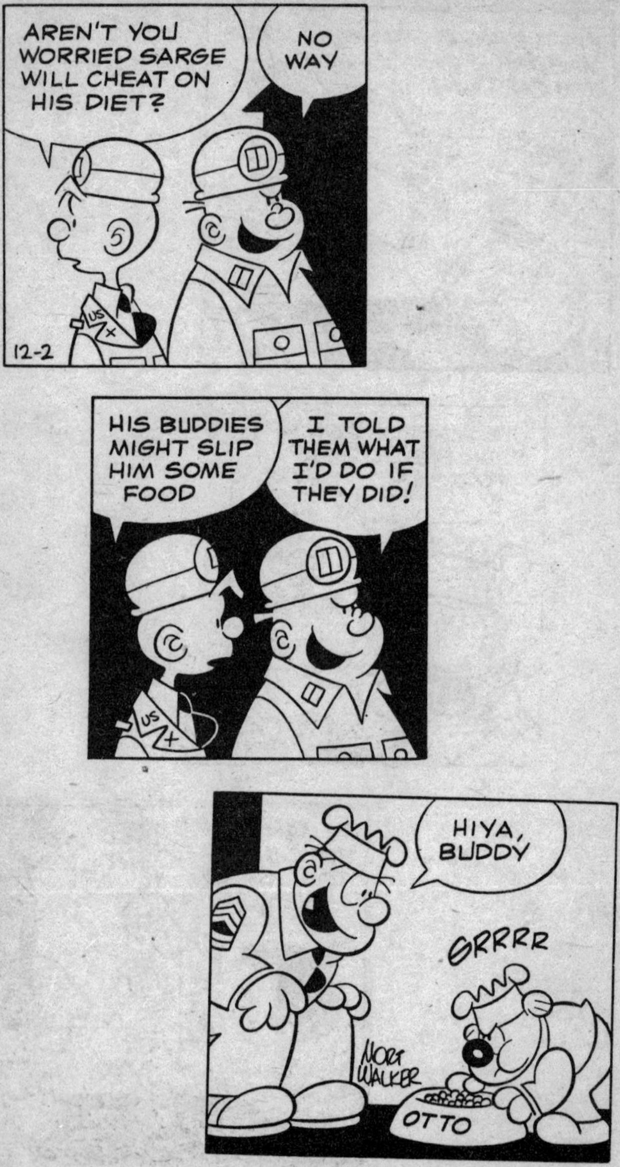
AREN'T YOU WORRIED SARGE WILL CHEAT ON HIS DIET?
NO WAY
12-2
HIS BUDDIES MIGHT SLIP HIM SOME FOOD
I TOLD THEM WHAT I'D DO IF THEY DID!
HIYA, BUDDY
GRRRR
MORT WALKER
OTTO

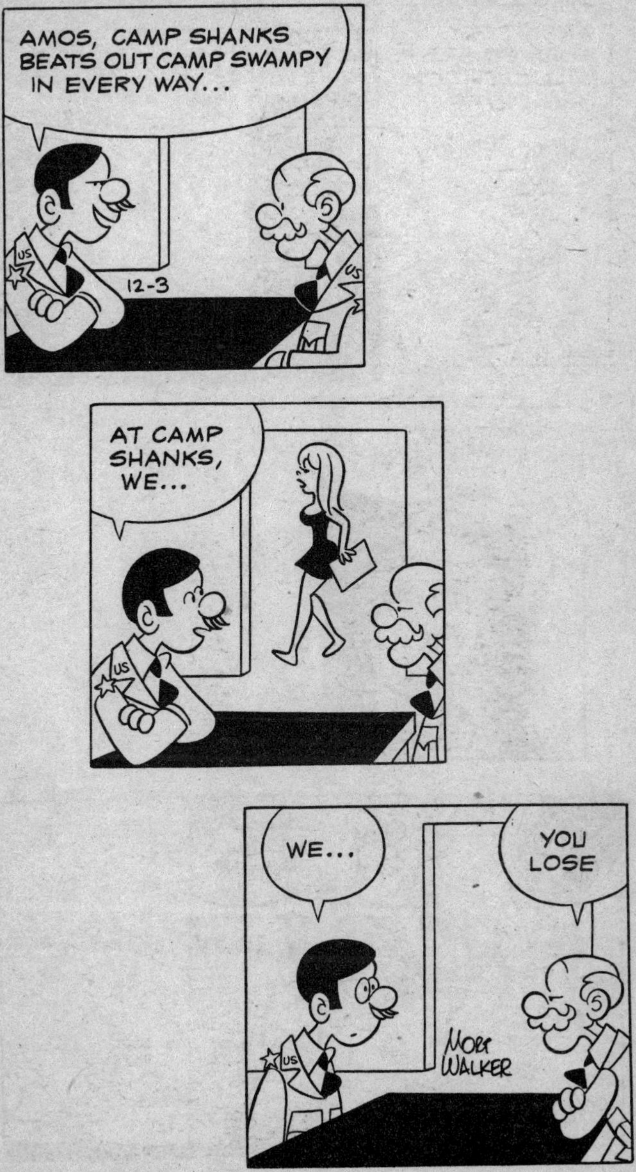
AMOS, CAMP SHANKS BEATS OUT CAMP SWAMPY IN EVERY WAY...
12-3
AT CAMP SHANKS, WE...
WE...
YOU LOSE
MORT WALKER

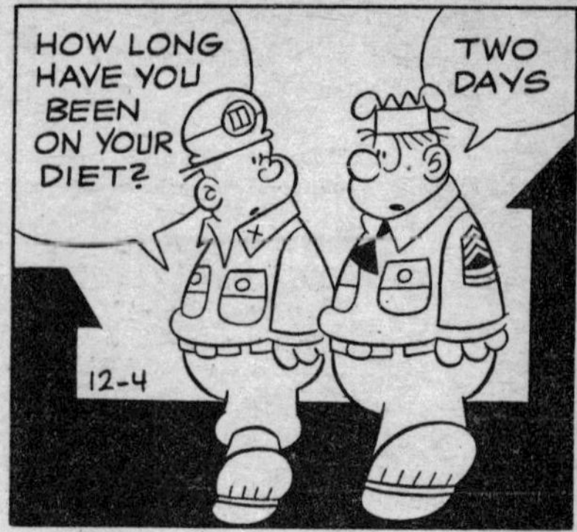
HOW LONG HAVE YOU BEEN ON YOUR DIET?
TWO DAYS
12-4

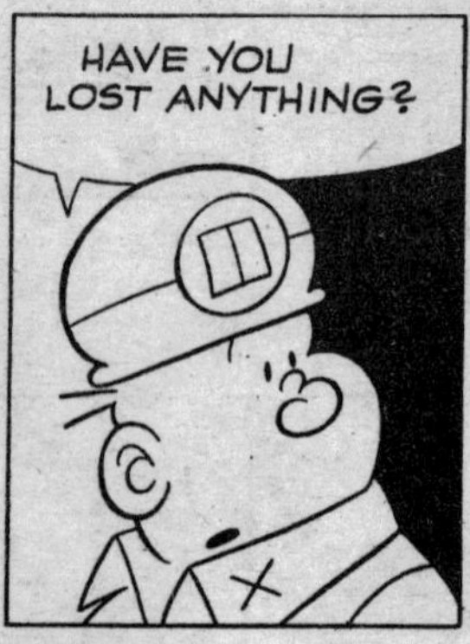
HAVE YOU LOST ANYTHING?

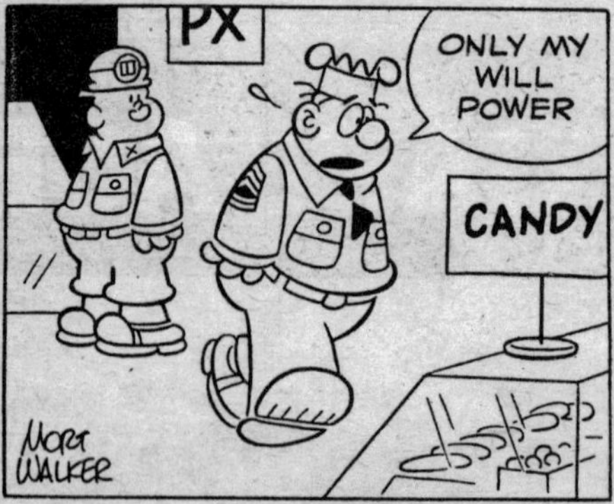
PX
ONLY MY WILL POWER
CANDY
MORT WALKER

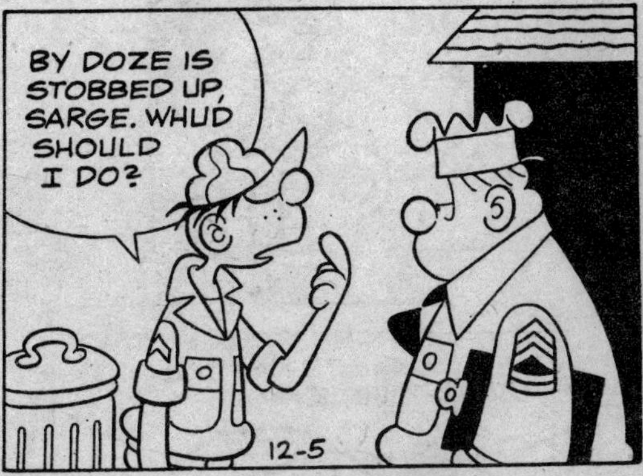
BY DOZE IS STOBBED UP, SARGE. WHUD SHOULD I DO?
12-5

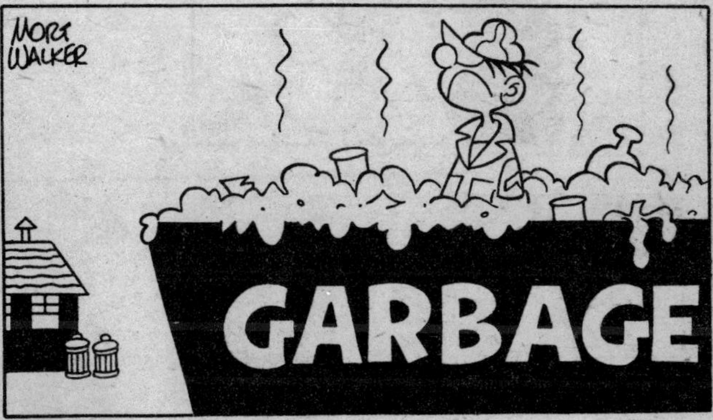
MORT WALKER
GARBAGE

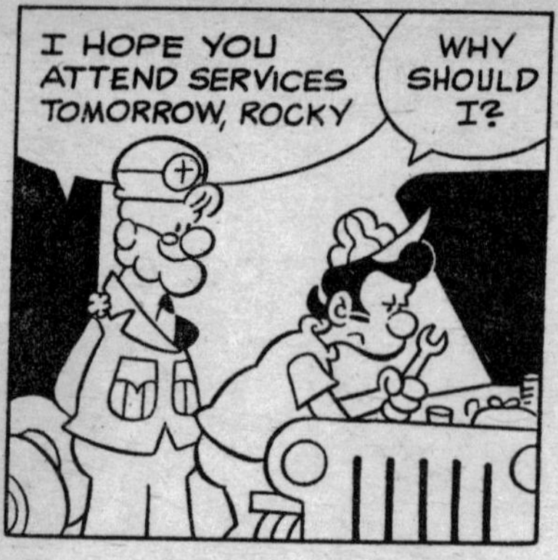
I HOPE YOU ATTEND SERVICES TOMORROW, ROCKY
WHY SHOULD I?

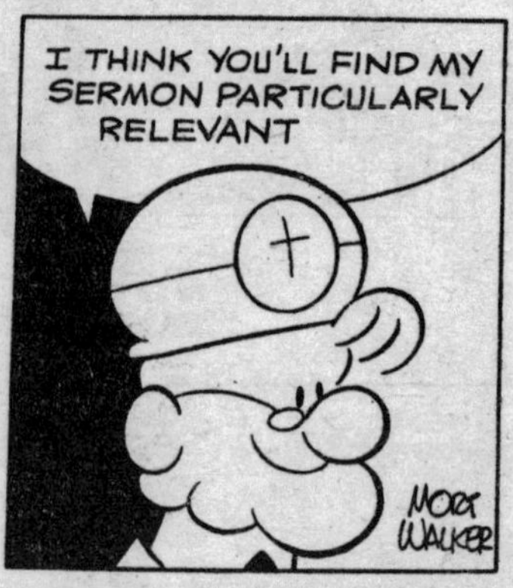
I THINK YOU'LL FIND MY SERMON PARTICULARLY RELEVANT
MORT WALKER

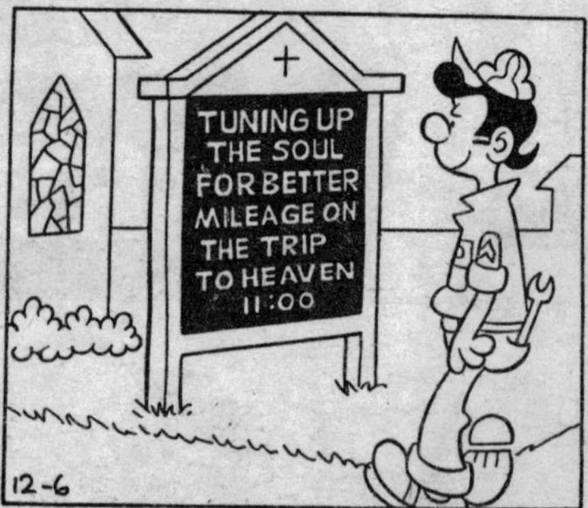
TUNING UP THE SOUL FOR BETTER MILEAGE ON THE TRIP TO HEAVEN 11:00
12-6

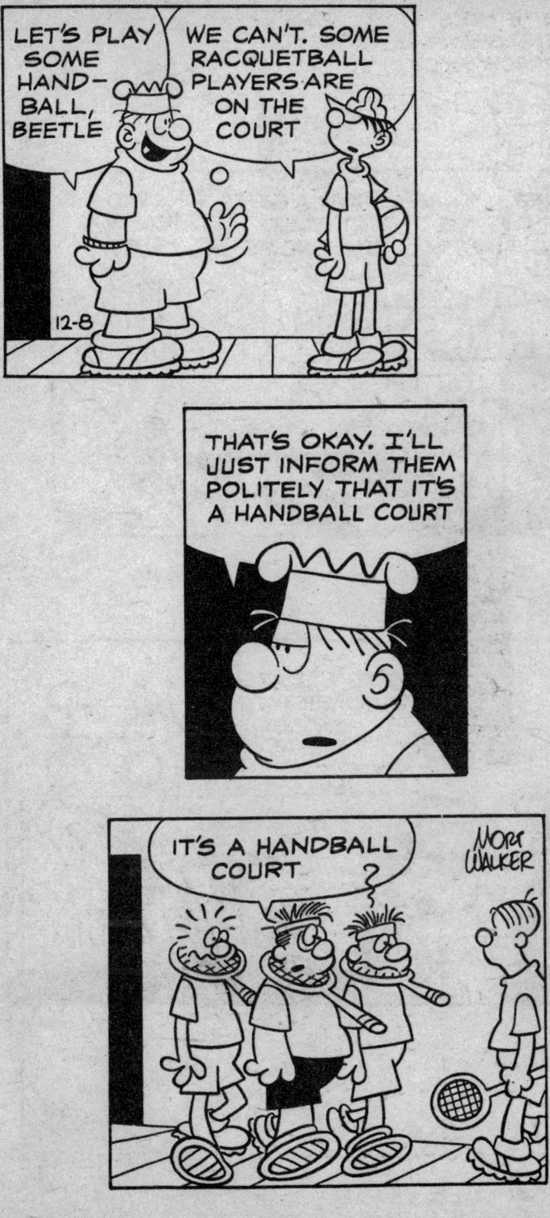
LET'S PLAY SOME HAND-BALL, BEETLE
WE CAN'T. SOME RACQUETBALL PLAYERS ARE ON THE COURT
12-8
THAT'S OKAY. I'LL JUST INFORM THEM POLITELY THAT IT'S A HANDBALL COURT
IT'S A HANDBALL COURT
?
MORT WALKER

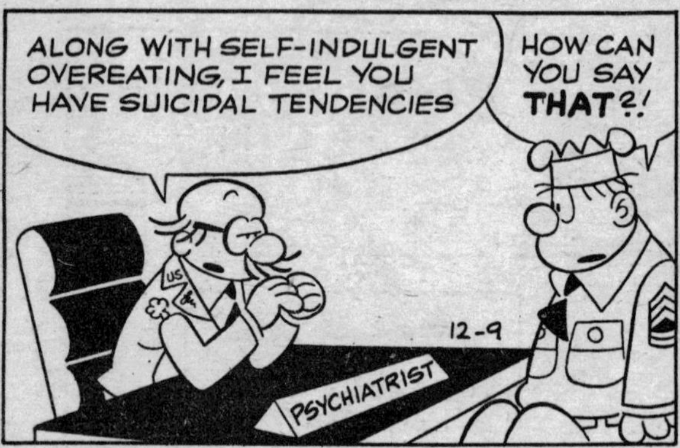
ALONG WITH SELF-INDULGENT OVEREATING, I FEEL YOU HAVE SUICIDAL TENDENCIES
HOW CAN YOU SAY **THAT**?!
12-9
PSYCHIATRIST

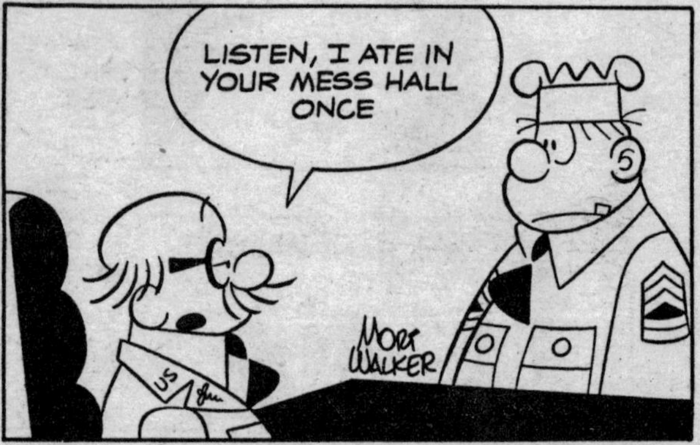
LISTEN, I ATE IN YOUR MESS HALL ONCE
MORT WALKER

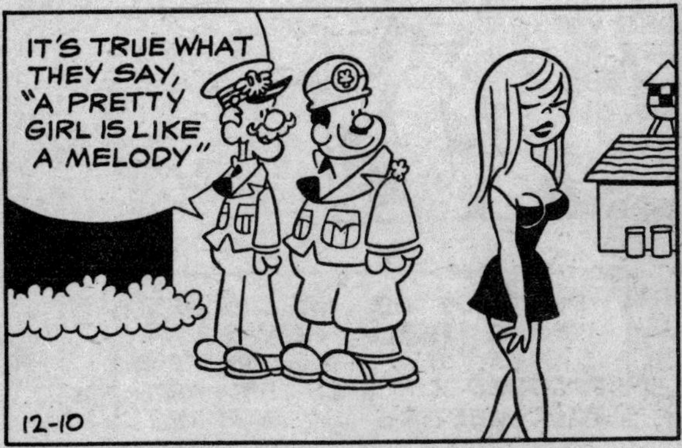
IT'S TRUE WHAT THEY SAY, "A PRETTY GIRL IS LIKE A MELODY"
12-10

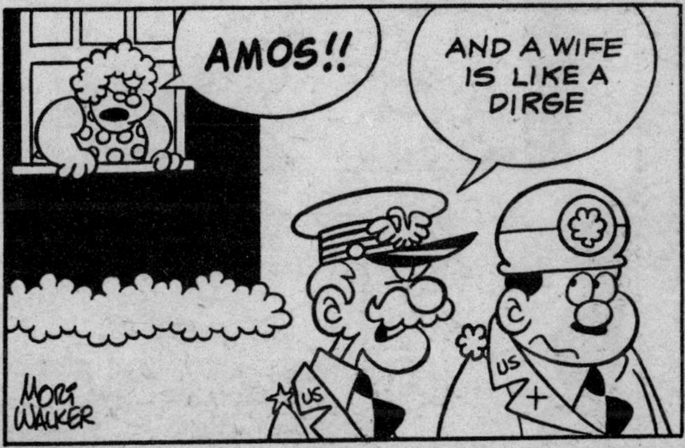
AMOS!!
AND A WIFE IS LIKE A DIRGE
MORT WALKER

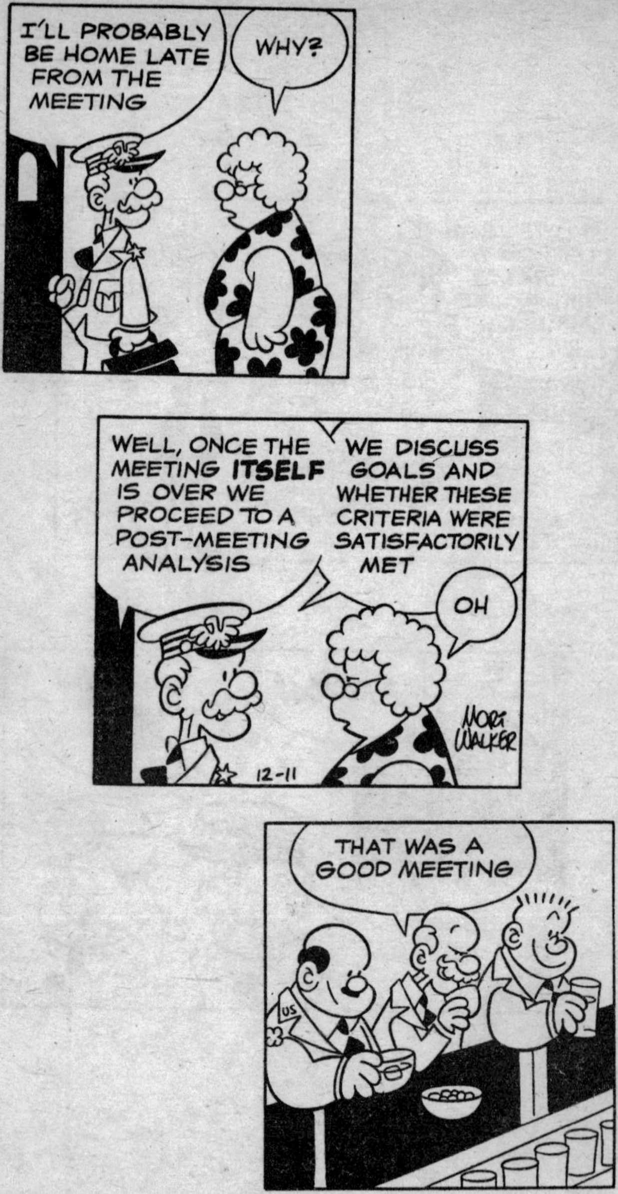
I'LL PROBABLY BE HOME LATE FROM THE MEETING
WHY?
WELL, ONCE THE MEETING **ITSELF** IS OVER WE PROCEED TO A POST-MEETING ANALYSIS
WE DISCUSS GOALS AND WHETHER THESE CRITERIA WERE SATISFACTORILY MET
OH
MORT WALKER
12-11
THAT WAS A GOOD MEETING
US

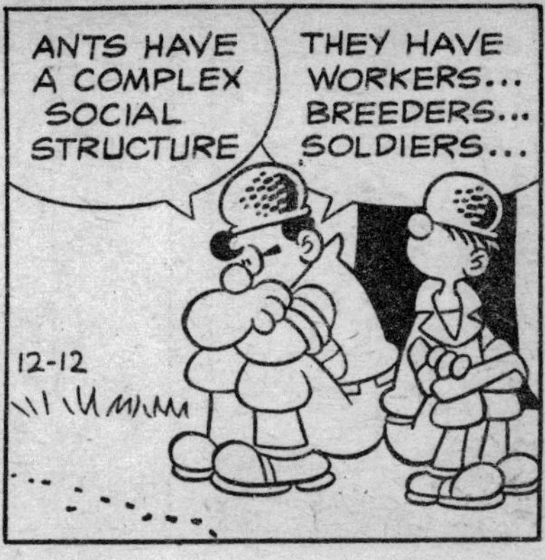
ANTS HAVE A COMPLEX SOCIAL STRUCTURE
THEY HAVE WORKERS... BREEDERS... SOLDIERS...
12-12

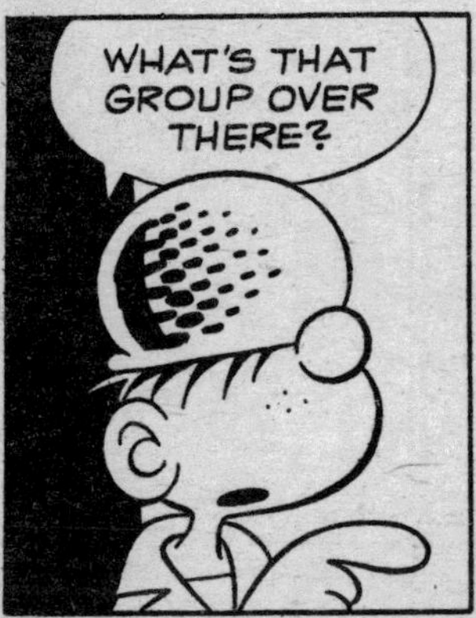
WHAT'S THAT GROUP OVER THERE?

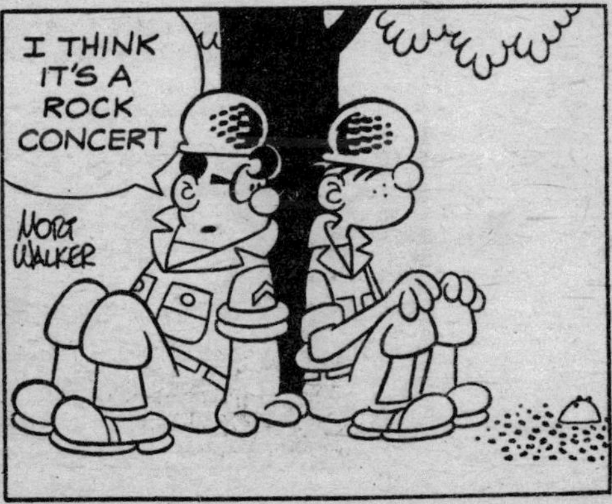
I THINK IT'S A ROCK CONCERT
MORT WALKER

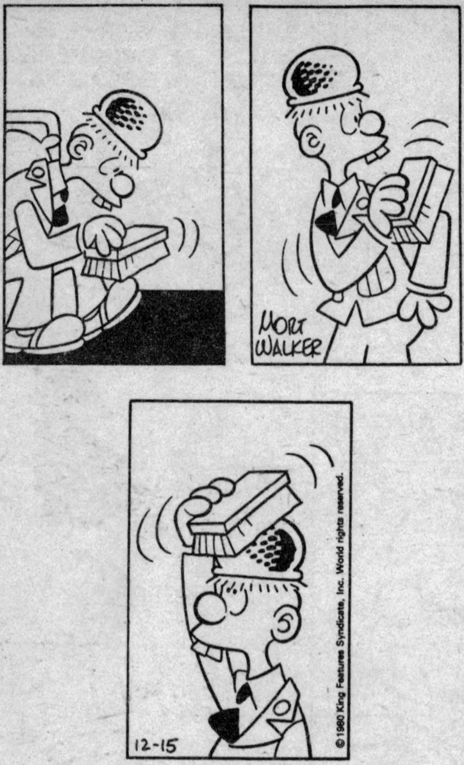
MORT WALKER
12-15
© 1980 King Features Syndicate, Inc. World rights reserved.

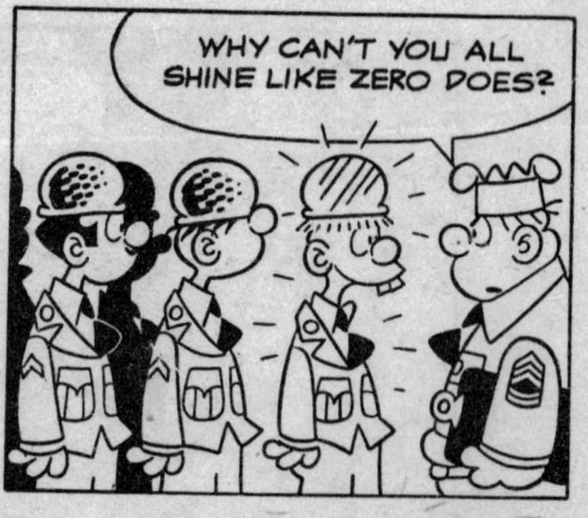
WHY CAN'T YOU ALL SHINE LIKE ZERO DOES?

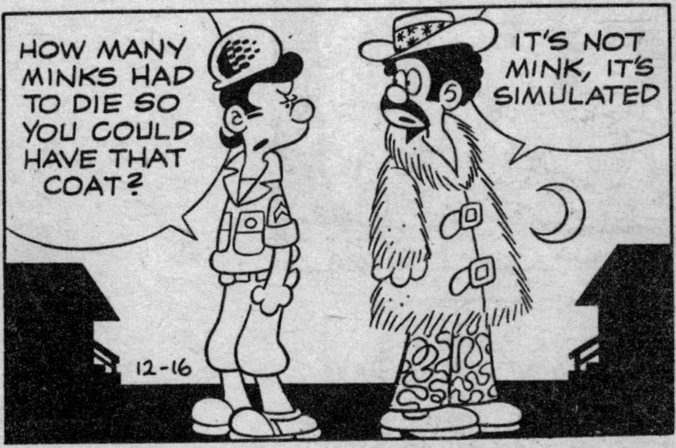
HOW MANY MINKS HAD TO DIE SO YOU COULD HAVE THAT COAT?
IT'S NOT MINK, IT'S SIMULATED
12-16

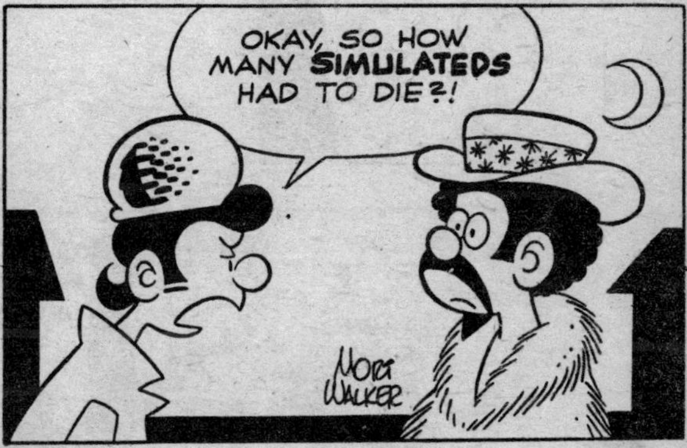
OKAY, SO HOW MANY **SIMULATEDS** HAD TO DIE?!
MORT WALKER

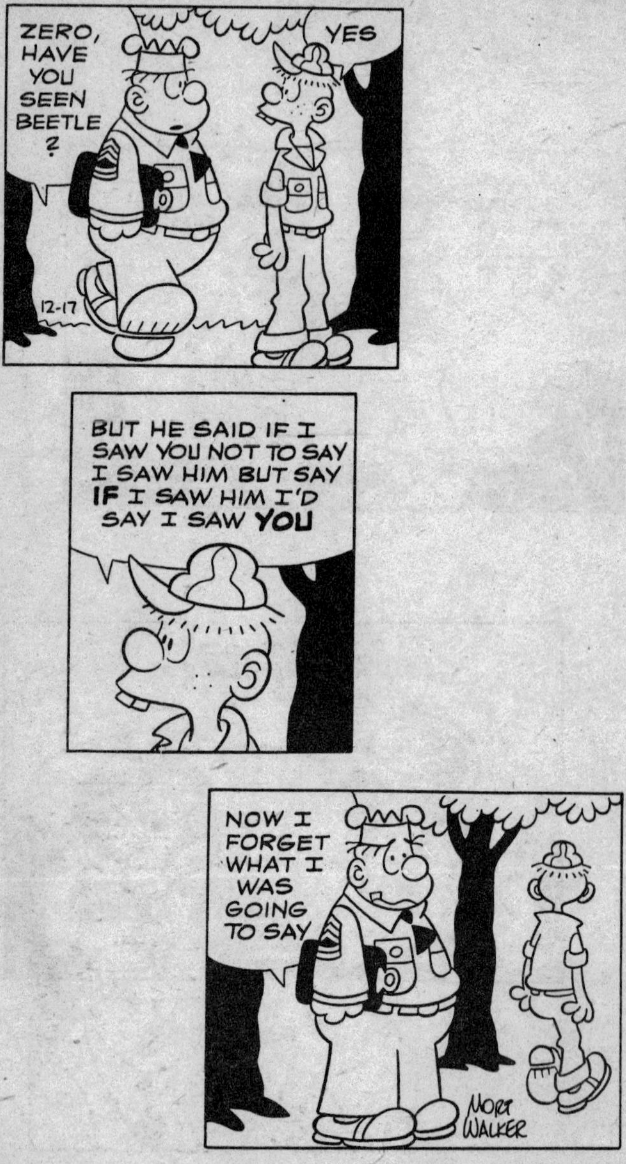
ZERO, HAVE YOU SEEN BEETLE ?
YES
12-17
BUT HE SAID IF I SAW YOU NOT TO SAY I SAW HIM BUT SAY IF I SAW HIM I'D SAY I SAW YOU
NOW I FORGET WHAT I WAS GOING TO SAY
MORT WALKER

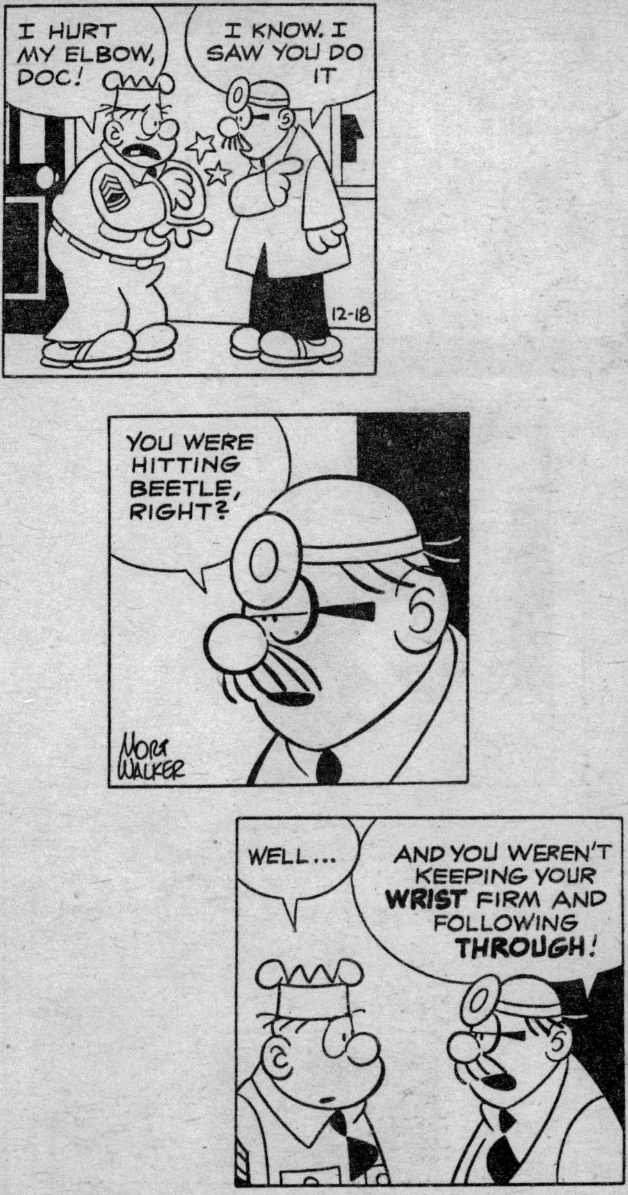

I HURT MY ELBOW, DOC!
I KNOW. I SAW YOU DO IT
12-18
YOU WERE HITTING BEETLE, RIGHT?
MORT WALKER
WELL...
AND YOU WEREN'T KEEPING YOUR WRIST FIRM AND FOLLOWING THROUGH!

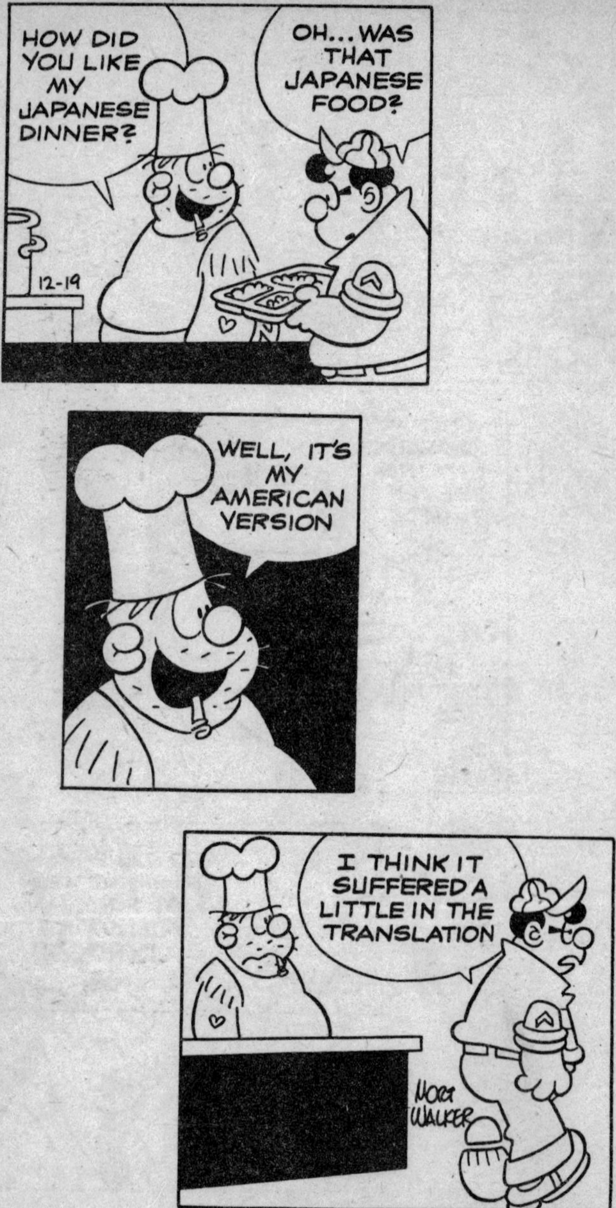
HOW DID YOU LIKE MY JAPANESE DINNER?
OH... WAS THAT JAPANESE FOOD?
12-19
WELL, IT'S MY AMERICAN VERSION
I THINK IT SUFFERED A LITTLE IN THE TRANSLATION
MORT WALKER

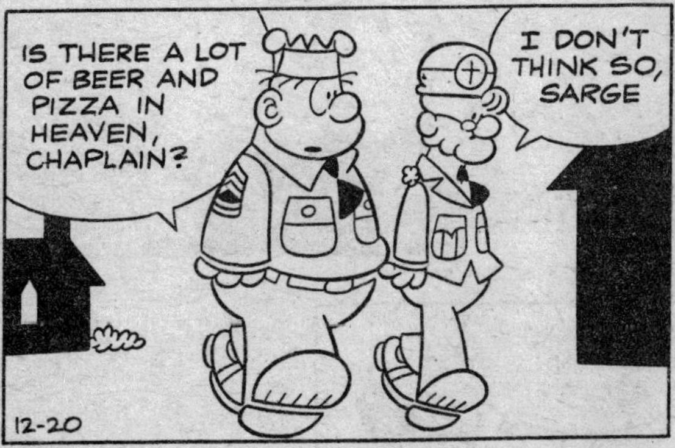
IS THERE A LOT OF BEER AND PIZZA IN HEAVEN, CHAPLAIN?
I DON'T THINK SO, SARGE
12-20

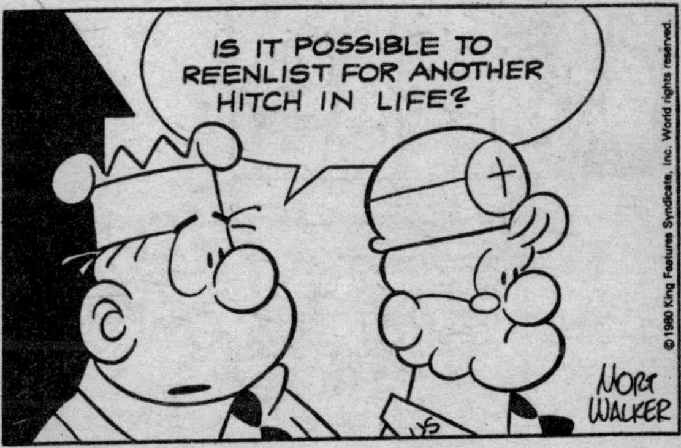
IS IT POSSIBLE TO REENLIST FOR ANOTHER HITCH IN LIFE?
© 1980 King Features Syndicate, Inc. World rights reserved.
MORT WALKER

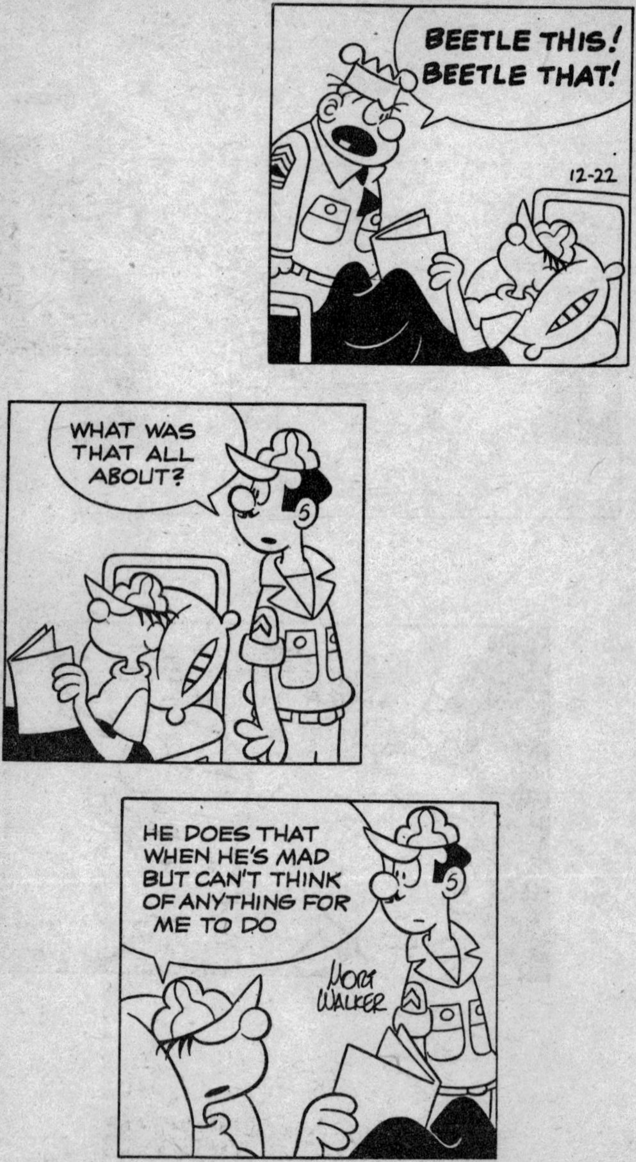
BEETLE THIS! BEETLE THAT!
12-22
WHAT WAS THAT ALL ABOUT?
HE DOES THAT WHEN HE'S MAD BUT CAN'T THINK OF ANYTHING FOR ME TO DO
MORT WALKER

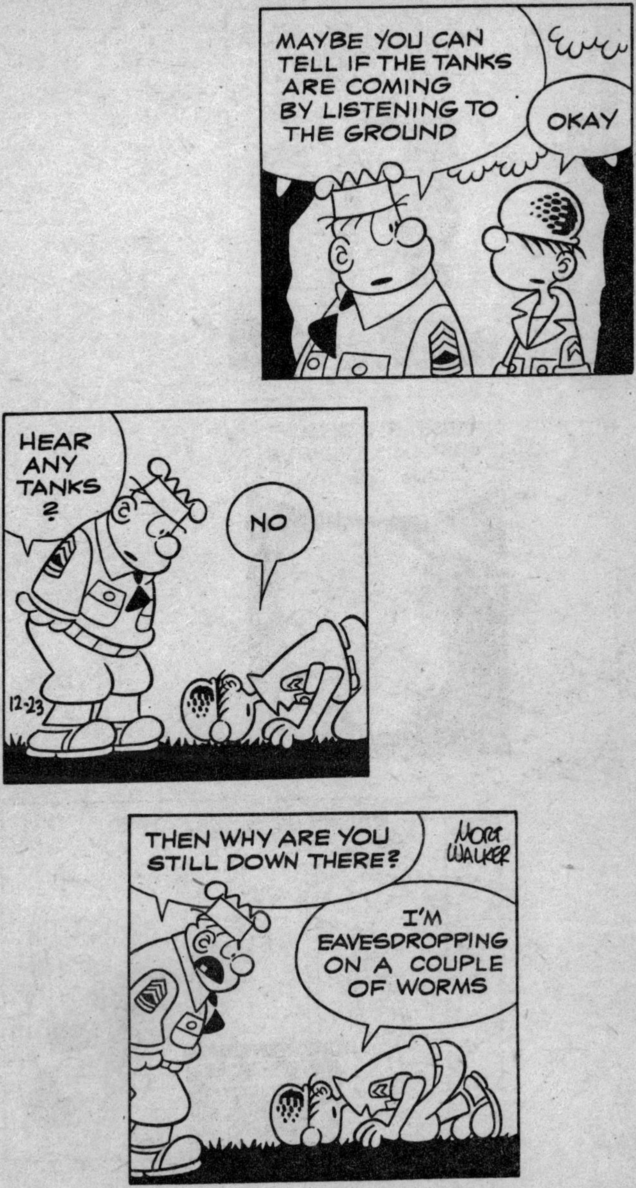
MAYBE YOU CAN TELL IF THE TANKS ARE COMING BY LISTENING TO THE GROUND
OKAY
HEAR ANY TANKS?
NO
12-23
THEN WHY ARE YOU STILL DOWN THERE?
MORT WALKER
I'M EAVESDROPPING ON A COUPLE OF WORMS

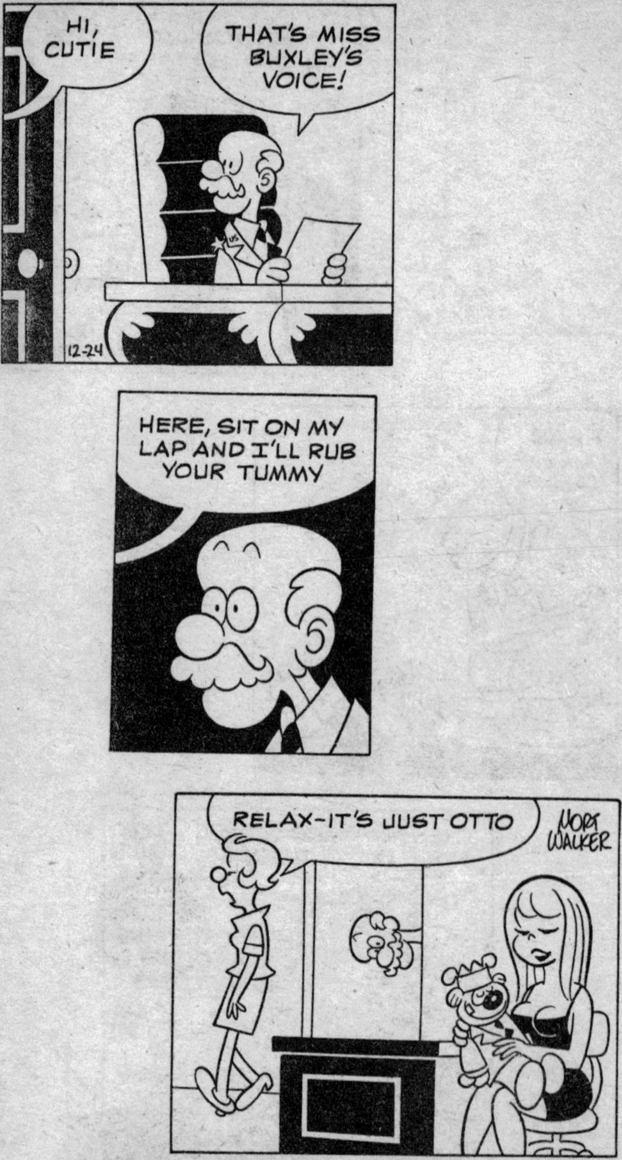
HI, CUTIE
THAT'S MISS BUXLEY'S VOICE!
12-24
HERE, SIT ON MY LAP AND I'LL RUB YOUR TUMMY
RELAX–IT'S JUST OTTO
MORT WALKER

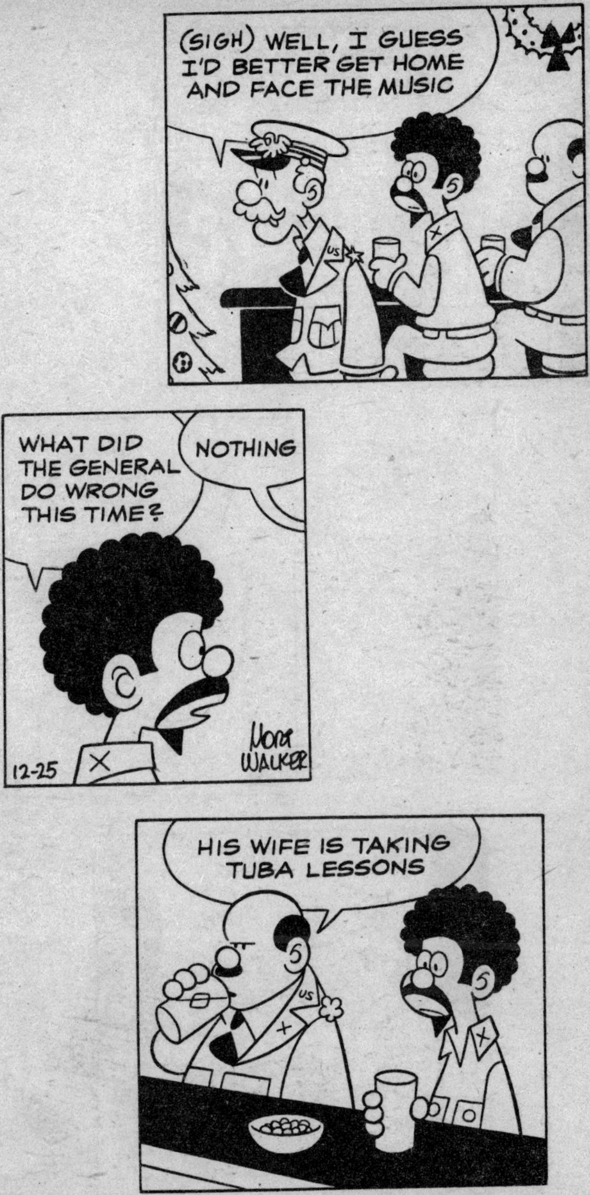
(SIGH) WELL, I GUESS I'D BETTER GET HOME AND FACE THE MUSIC
WHAT DID THE GENERAL DO WRONG THIS TIME?
NOTHING
12-25
MORT WALKER
HIS WIFE IS TAKING TUBA LESSONS

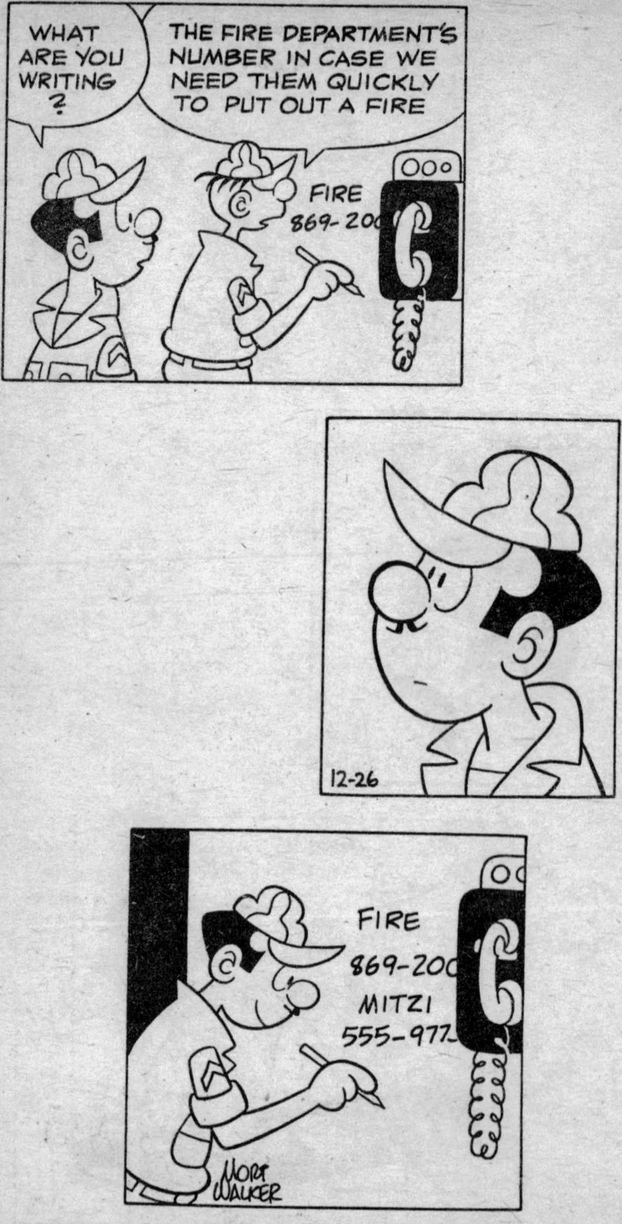
WHAT ARE YOU WRITING ?
THE FIRE DEPARTMENT'S NUMBER IN CASE WE NEED THEM QUICKLY TO PUT OUT A FIRE
FIRE
869-20
12-26
FIRE
869-20
MITZI
555-977
MORT WALKER

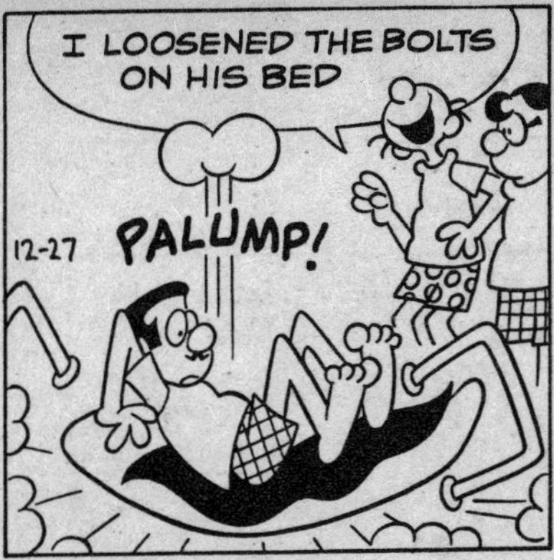
I LOOSENED THE BOLTS ON HIS BED
PALUMP!
12-27

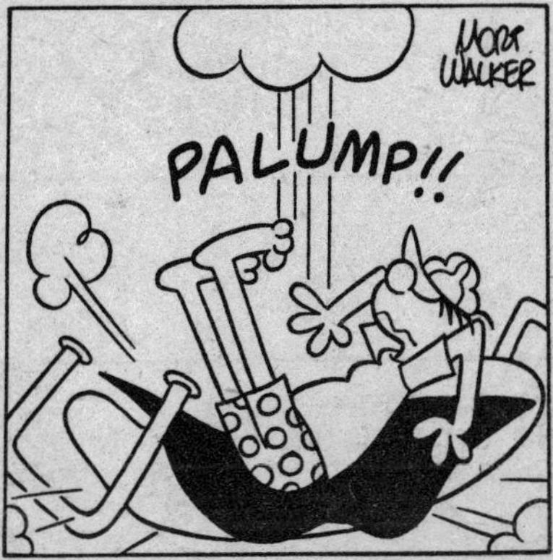
MORT WALKER
PALUMP!!

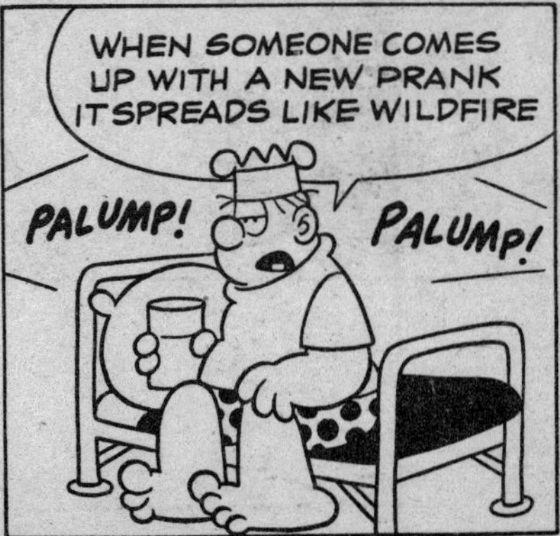
WHEN SOMEONE COMES UP WITH A NEW PRANK IT SPREADS LIKE WILDFIRE
PALUMP!
PALUMP!

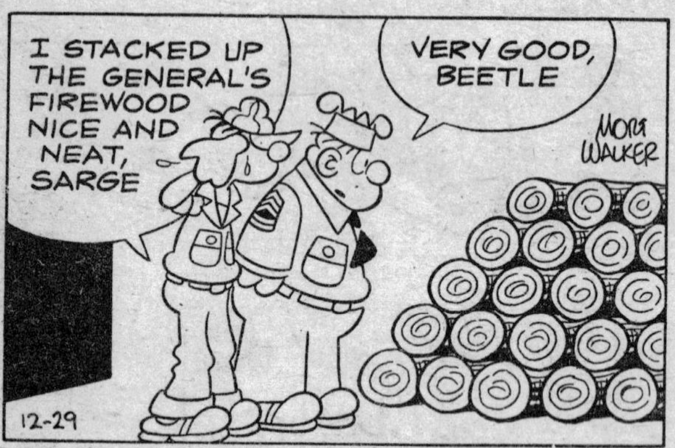
I STACKED UP THE GENERAL'S FIREWOOD NICE AND NEAT, SARGE
VERY GOOD, BEETLE
MORT WALKER
12-29

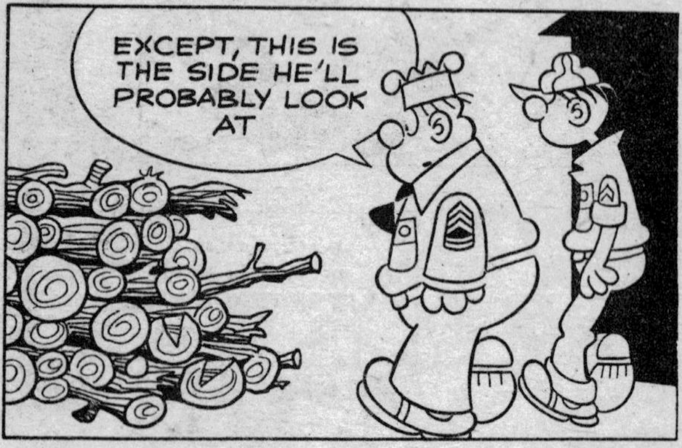
EXCEPT, THIS IS THE SIDE HE'LL PROBABLY LOOK AT

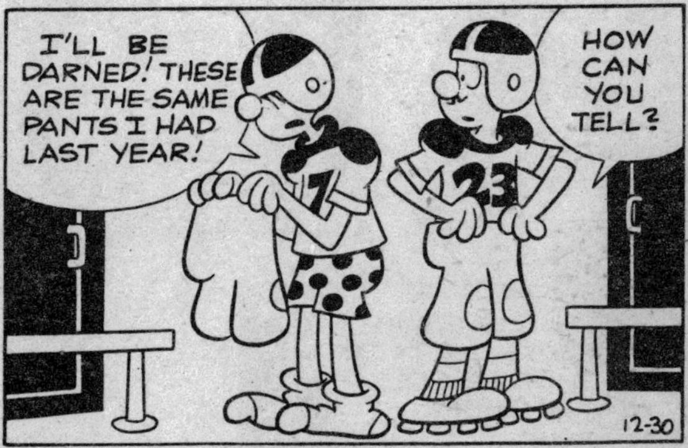
I'LL BE DARNED! THESE ARE THE SAME PANTS I HAD LAST YEAR!
HOW CAN YOU TELL?
7
23
12-30

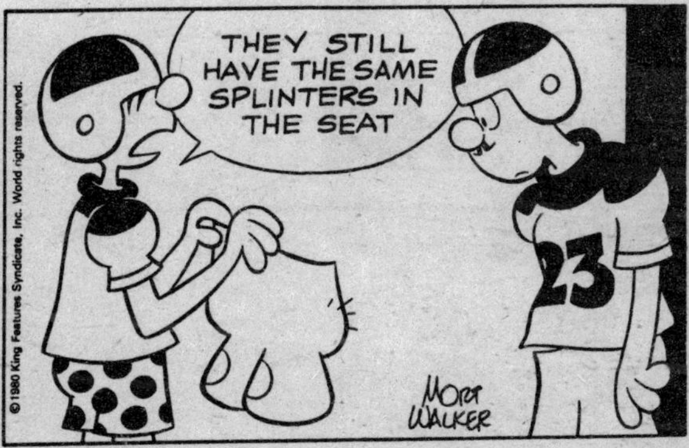
THEY STILL HAVE THE SAME SPLINTERS IN THE SEAT
23
MORT WALKER

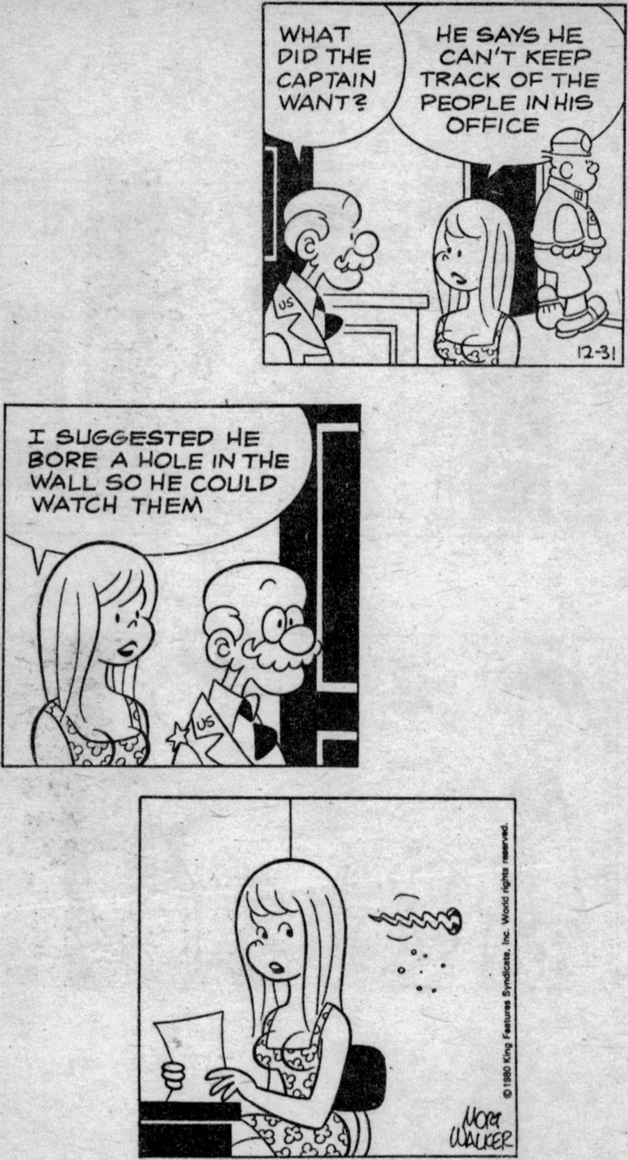
WHAT DID THE CAPTAIN WANT?
HE SAYS HE CAN'T KEEP TRACK OF THE PEOPLE IN HIS OFFICE
12-31
I SUGGESTED HE BORE A HOLE IN THE WALL SO HE COULD WATCH THEM
© 1980 King Features Syndicate, Inc. World rights reserved.
MORT WALKER

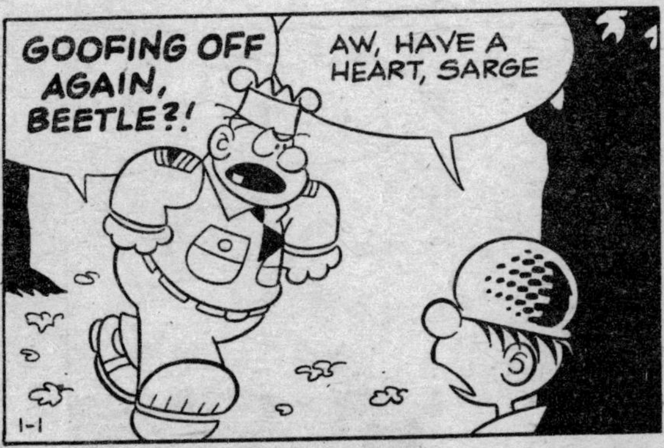
GOOFING OFF AGAIN, BEETLE?!
AW, HAVE A HEART, SARGE
1-1

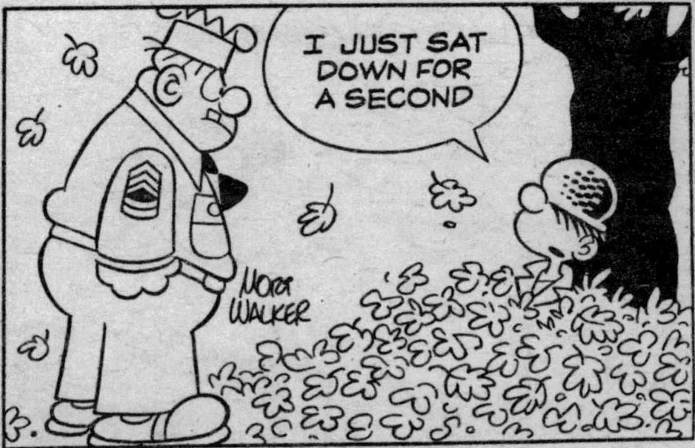
I JUST SAT DOWN FOR A SECOND
MORT WALKER

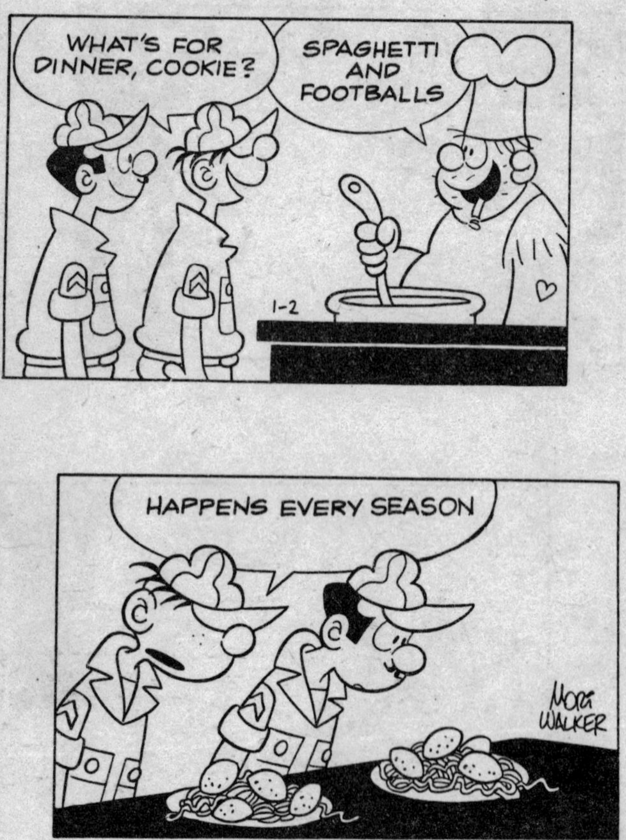
WHAT'S FOR DINNER, COOKIE?
SPAGHETTI AND FOOTBALLS
1-2
HAPPENS EVERY SEASON
MORT WALKER

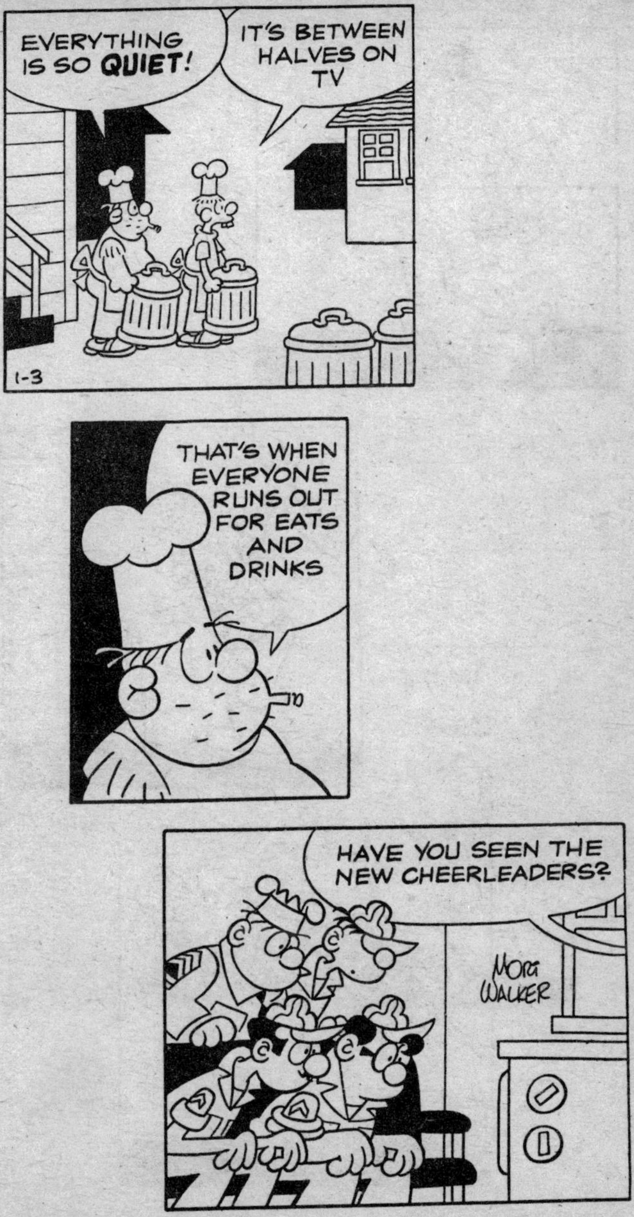
EVERYTHING IS SO **QUIET**!
IT'S BETWEEN HALVES ON TV
1-3
THAT'S WHEN EVERYONE RUNS OUT FOR EATS AND DRINKS
HAVE YOU SEEN THE NEW CHEERLEADERS?
MORT WALKER

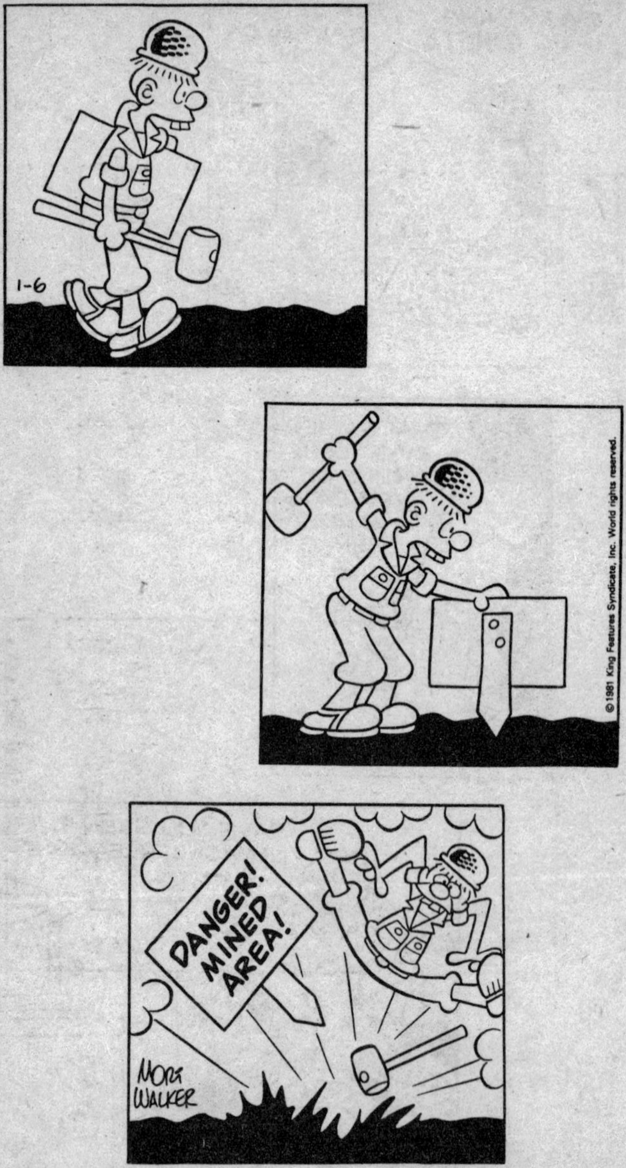
1-6
© 1981 King Features Syndicate, Inc. World rights reserved.
DANGER! MINED AREA!
MORT WALKER

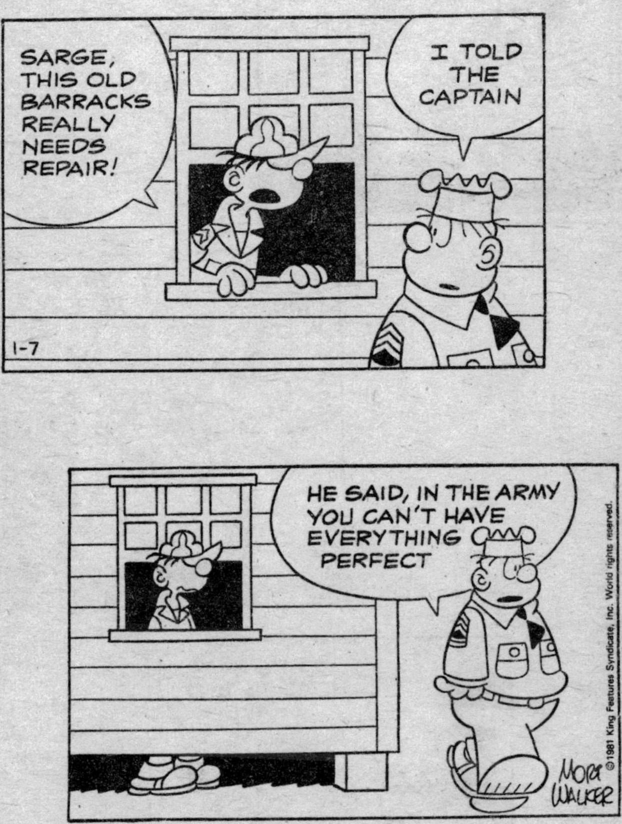
SARGE, THIS OLD BARRACKS REALLY NEEDS REPAIR!
I TOLD THE CAPTAIN
1-7
HE SAID, IN THE ARMY YOU CAN'T HAVE EVERYTHING PERFECT
©1981 King Features Syndicate, Inc. World rights reserved.
MORT WALKER

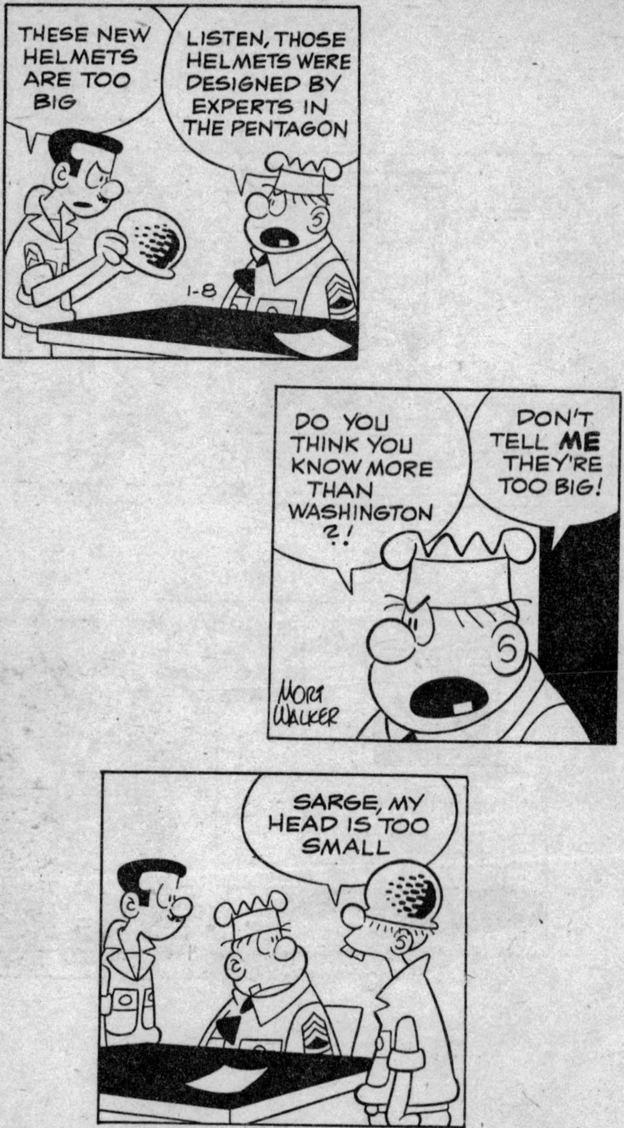
THESE NEW HELMETS ARE TOO BIG
LISTEN, THOSE HELMETS WERE DESIGNED BY EXPERTS IN THE PENTAGON
1-8
DO YOU THINK YOU KNOW MORE THAN WASHINGTON ?!
DON'T TELL **ME** THEY'RE TOO BIG!
MORT WALKER
SARGE, MY HEAD IS TOO SMALL

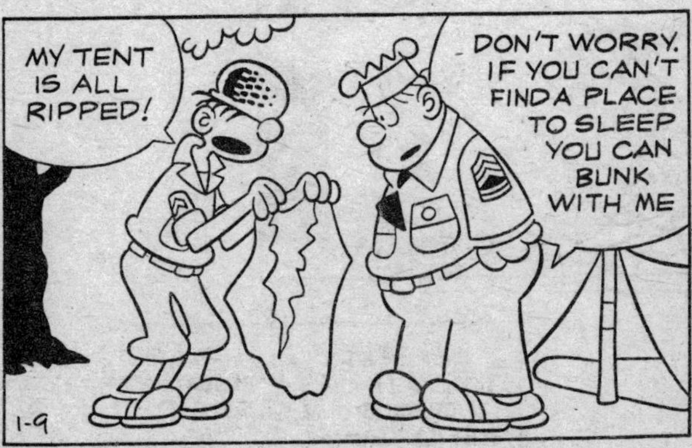
MY TENT IS ALL RIPPED!
DON'T WORRY. IF YOU CAN'T FINDA PLACE TO SLEEP YOU CAN BUNK WITH ME
1-9

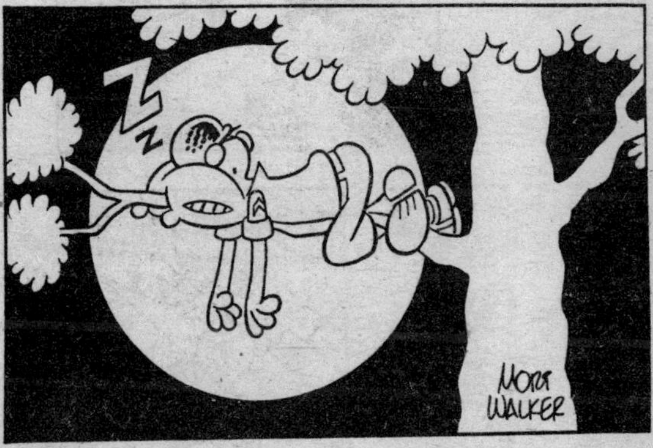
Z Z
MORT WALKER

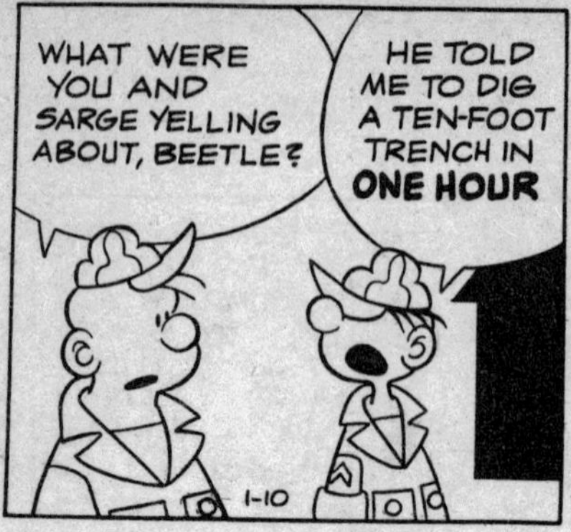
WHAT WERE YOU AND SARGE YELLING ABOUT, BEETLE?
HE TOLD ME TO DIG A TEN-FOOT TRENCH IN **ONE HOUR**
1-10

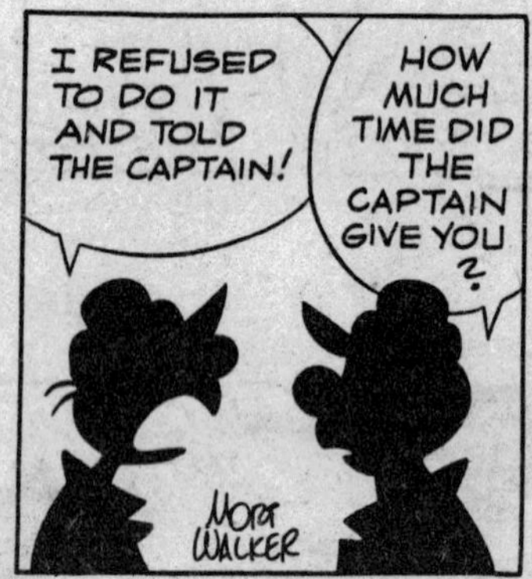
I REFUSED TO DO IT AND TOLD THE CAPTAIN!
HOW MUCH TIME DID THE CAPTAIN GIVE YOU?
MORT WALKER

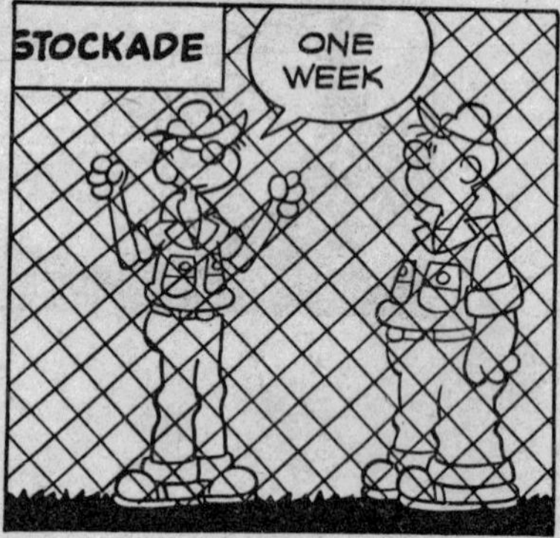
STOCKADE
ONE WEEK

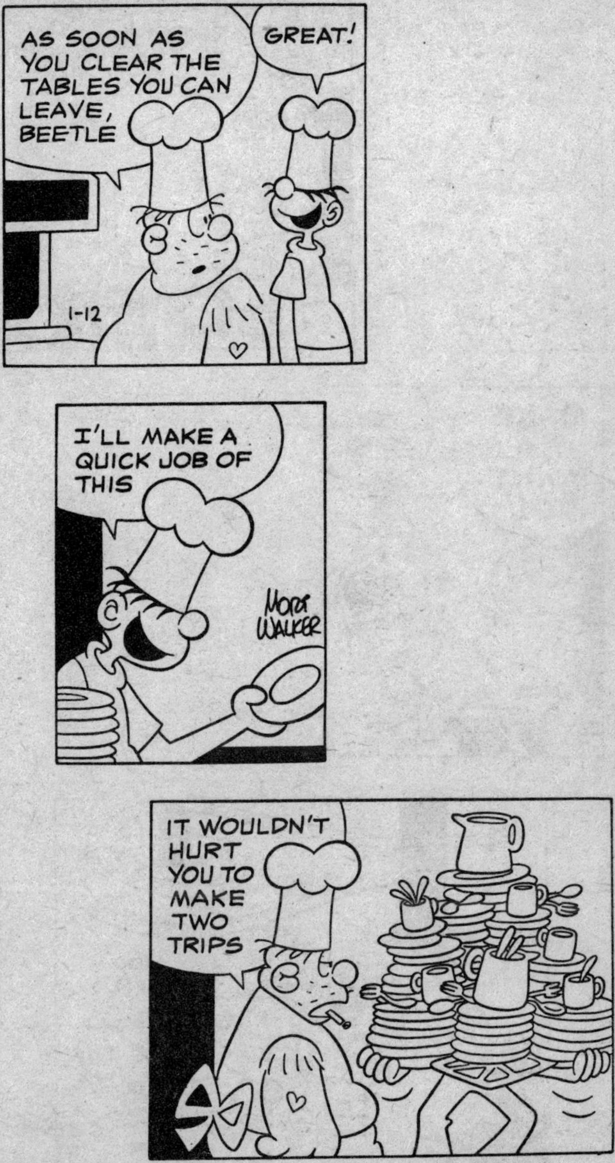
AS SOON AS YOU CLEAR THE TABLES YOU CAN LEAVE, BEETLE
GREAT!
1-12
I'LL MAKE A QUICK JOB OF THIS
MORT WALKER
IT WOULDN'T HURT YOU TO MAKE TWO TRIPS

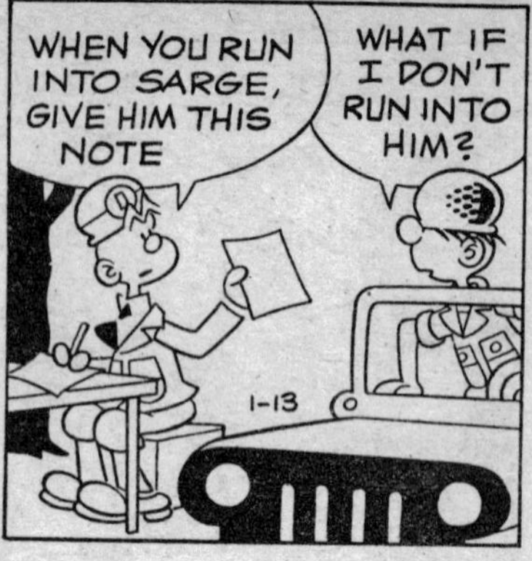
WHEN YOU RUN INTO SARGE, GIVE HIM THIS NOTE
WHAT IF I DON'T RUN INTO HIM?
1-13

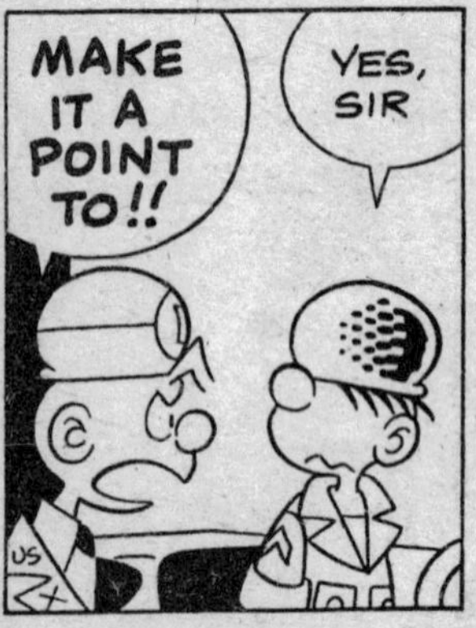
MAKE IT A POINT TO!!
YES, SIR

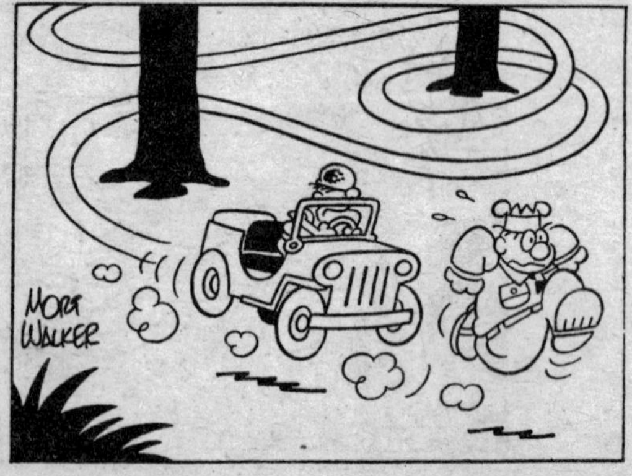
MORT WALKER

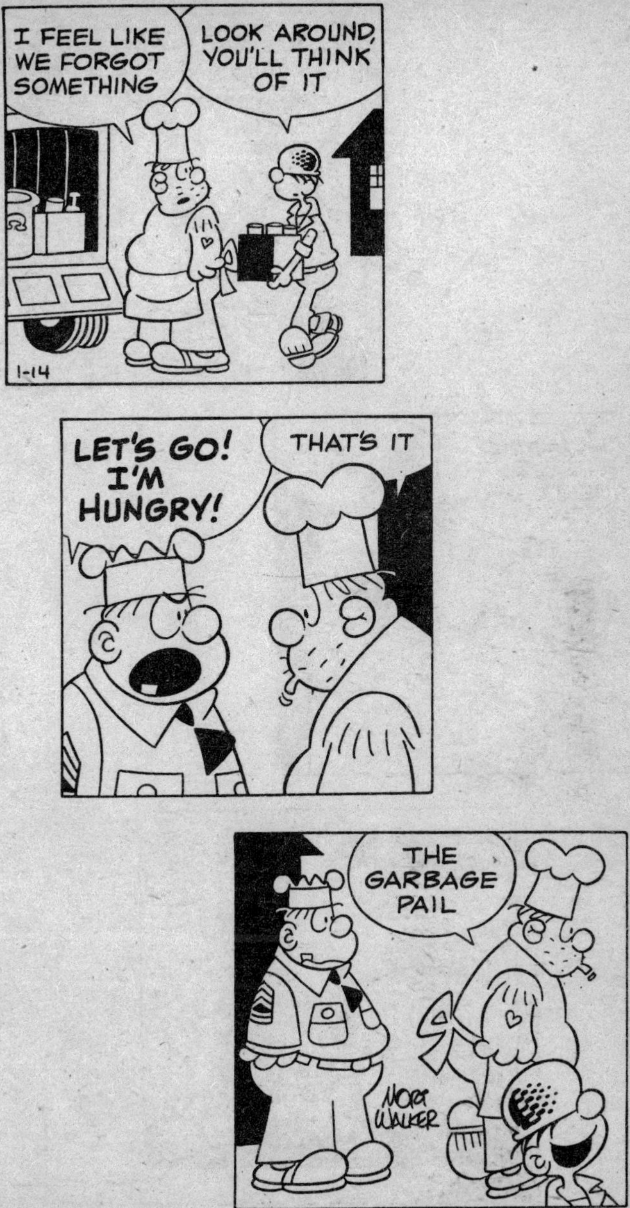
I FEEL LIKE WE FORGOT SOMETHING
LOOK AROUND, YOU'LL THINK OF IT
1-14
LET'S GO! I'M HUNGRY!
THAT'S IT
THE GARBAGE PAIL
MORT WALKER

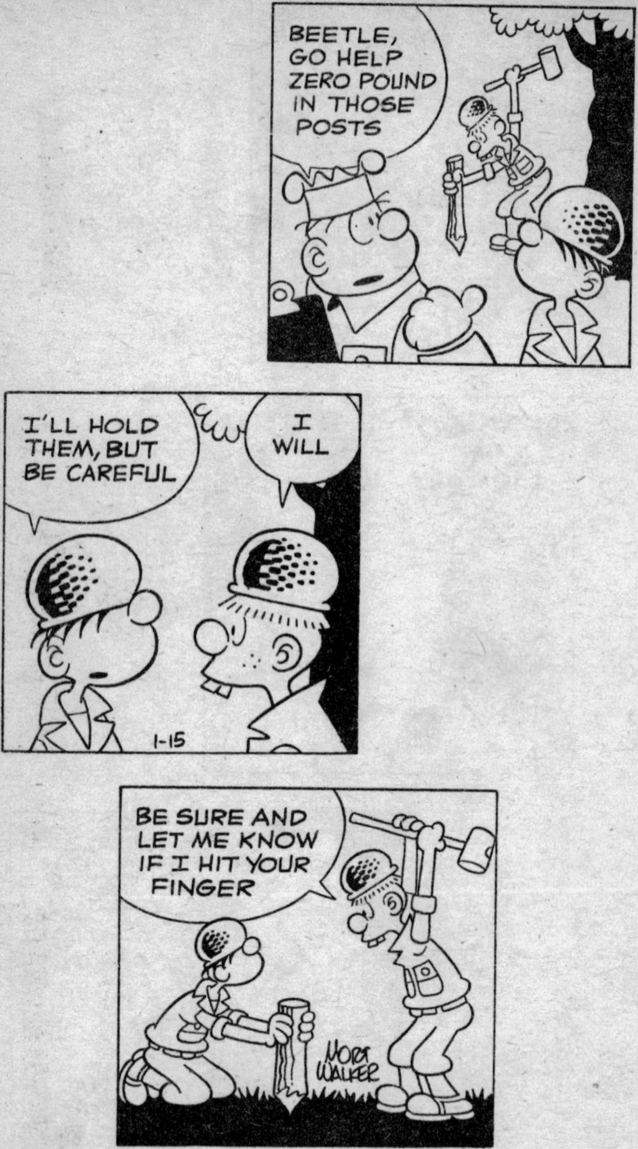

BEETLE, GO HELP ZERO POUND IN THOSE POSTS
I'LL HOLD THEM, BUT BE CAREFUL
I WILL
1-15
BE SURE AND LET ME KNOW IF I HIT YOUR FINGER
MORT WALKER

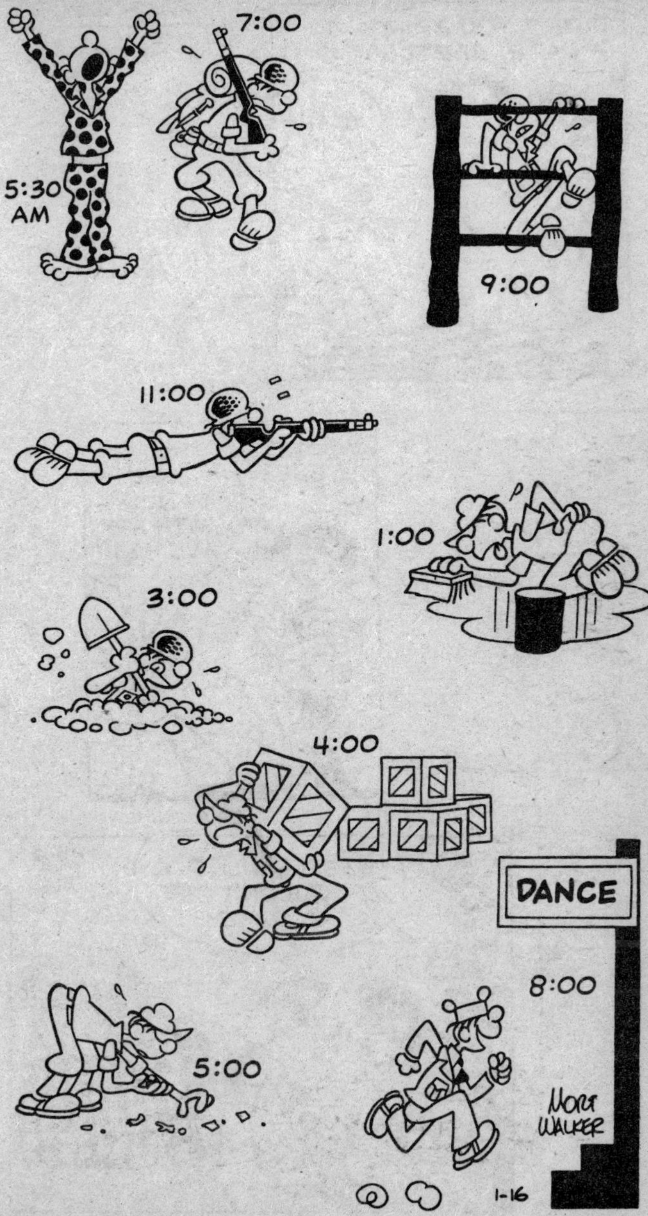
5:30 AM
7:00
9:00
11:00
1:00
3:00
4:00
DANCE
5:00
8:00
MORT WALKER
1-16

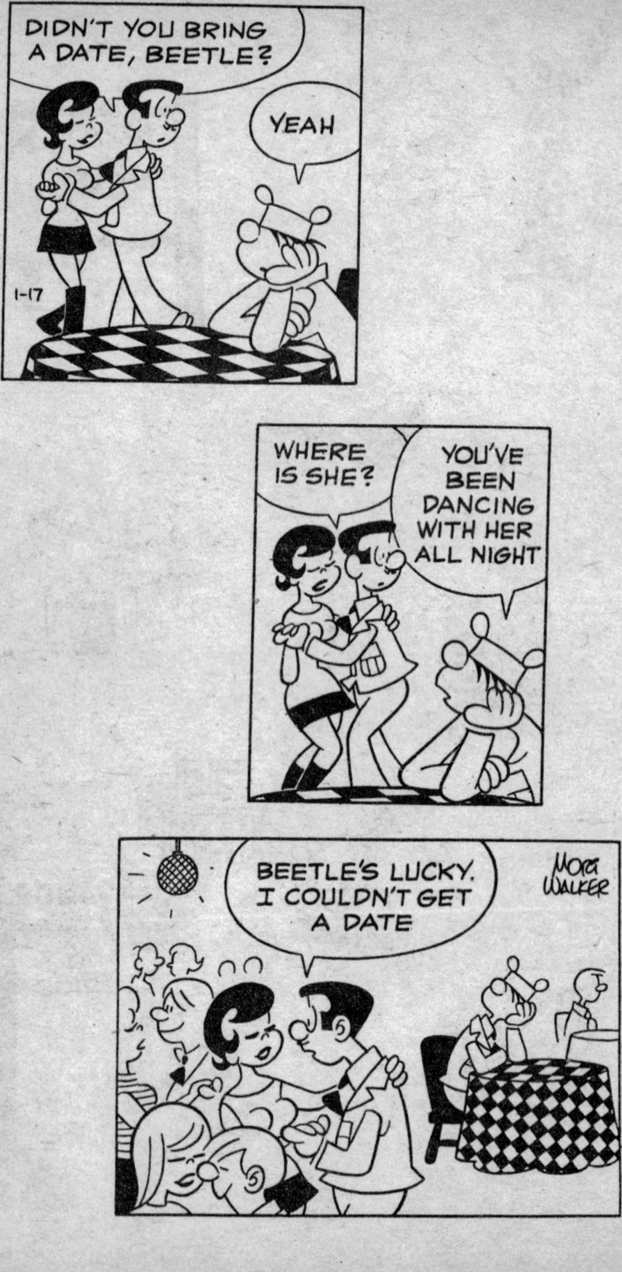
DIDN'T YOU BRING A DATE, BEETLE?
YEAH
1-17
WHERE IS SHE?
YOU'VE BEEN DANCING WITH HER ALL NIGHT
BEETLE'S LUCKY. I COULDN'T GET A DATE
MORT WALKER

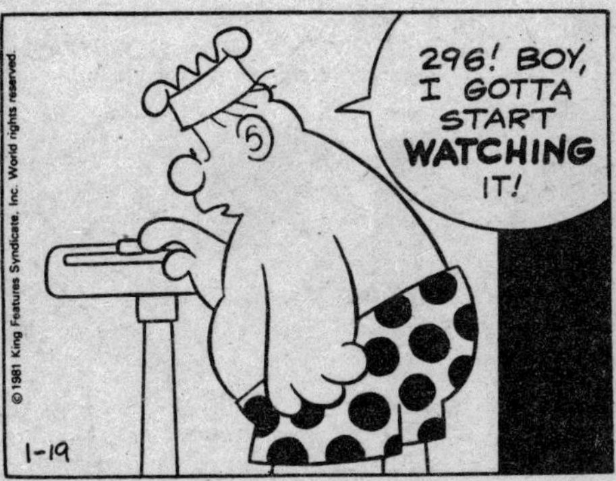
© 1981 King Features Syndicate, Inc. World rights reserved.
296! BOY, I GOTTA START **WATCHING** IT!
1-19

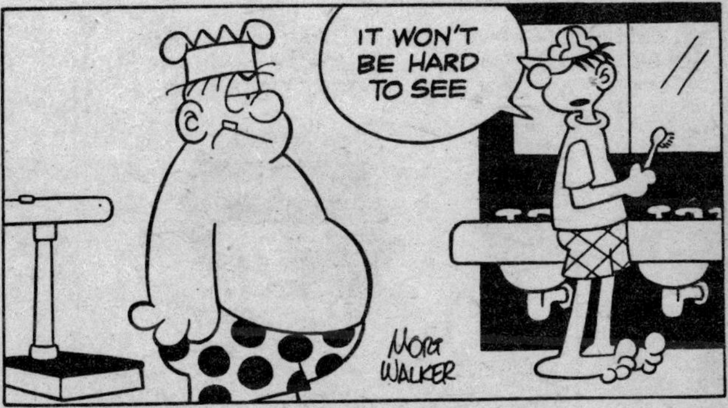
IT WON'T BE HARD TO SEE
MORT WALKER

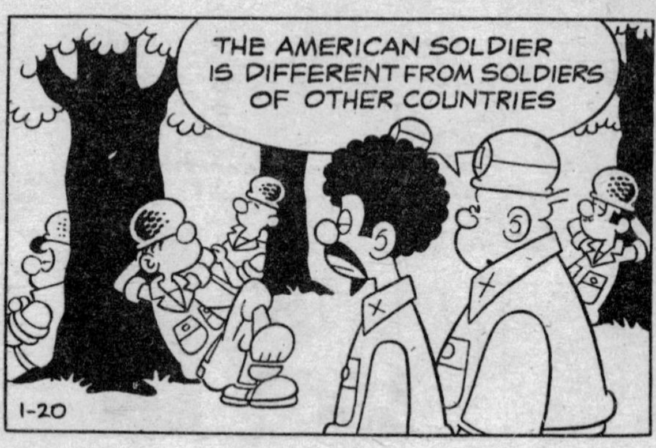
THE AMERICAN SOLDIER IS DIFFERENT FROM SOLDIERS OF OTHER COUNTRIES
1-20

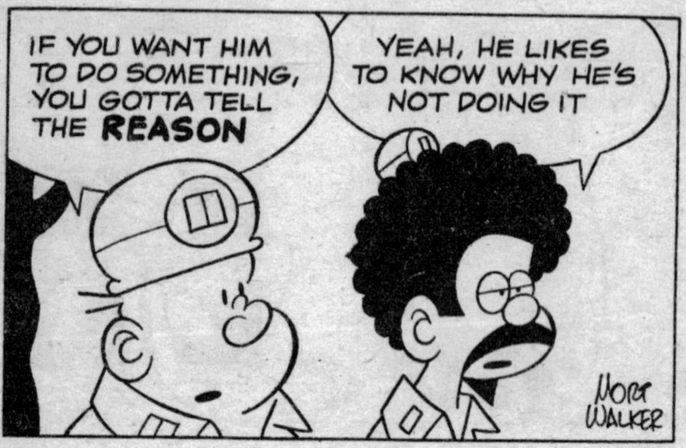
IF YOU WANT HIM TO DO SOMETHING, YOU GOTTA TELL THE **REASON**
YEAH, HE LIKES TO KNOW WHY HE'S NOT DOING IT
MORT WALKER

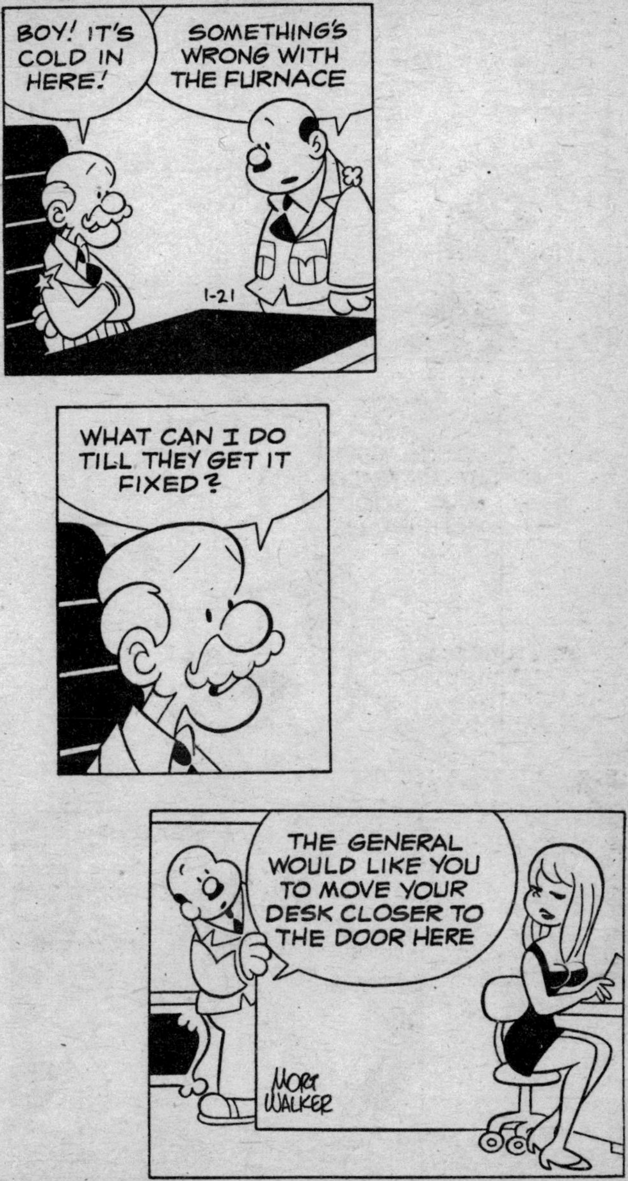
BOY! IT'S COLD IN HERE!
SOMETHING'S WRONG WITH THE FURNACE
1-21
WHAT CAN I DO TILL THEY GET IT FIXED?
THE GENERAL WOULD LIKE YOU TO MOVE YOUR DESK CLOSER TO THE DOOR HERE
MORT WALKER

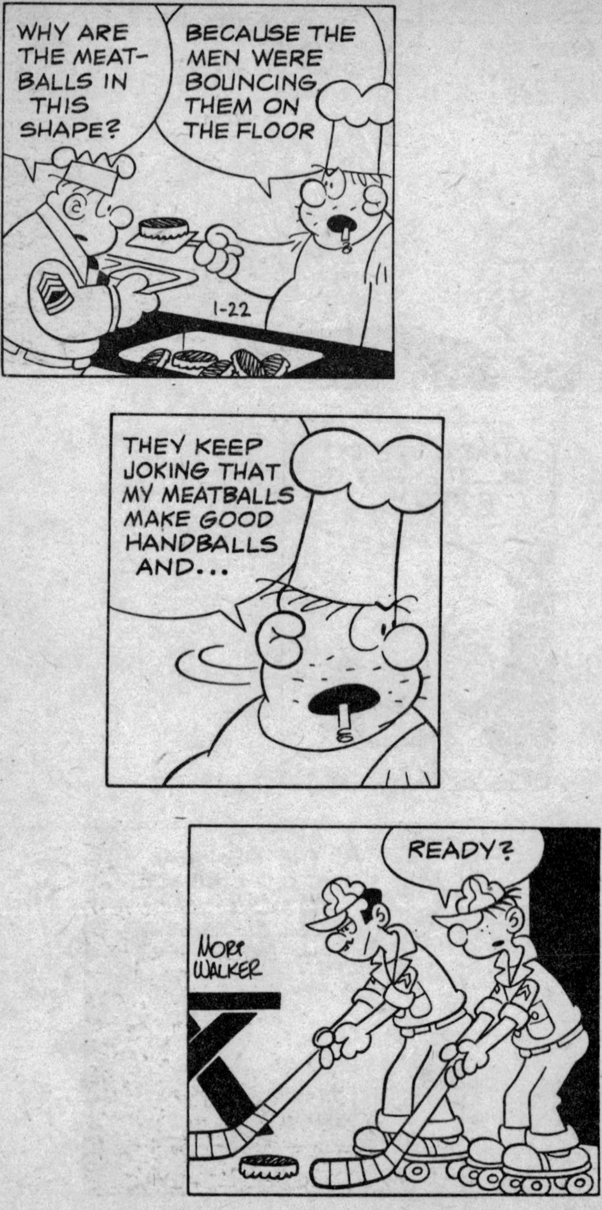
WHY ARE THE MEAT-BALLS IN THIS SHAPE?
BECAUSE THE MEN WERE BOUNCING THEM ON THE FLOOR
1-22
THEY KEEP JOKING THAT MY MEATBALLS MAKE GOOD HANDBALLS AND...
READY?
MORT WALKER

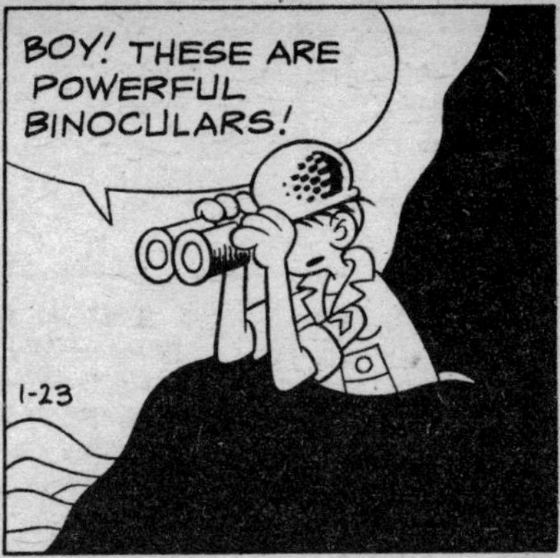
BOY! THESE ARE POWERFUL BINOCULARS!
1-23

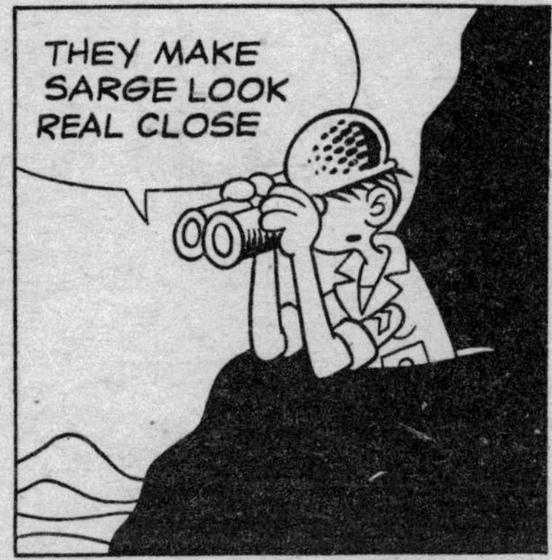
THEY MAKE SARGE LOOK REAL CLOSE

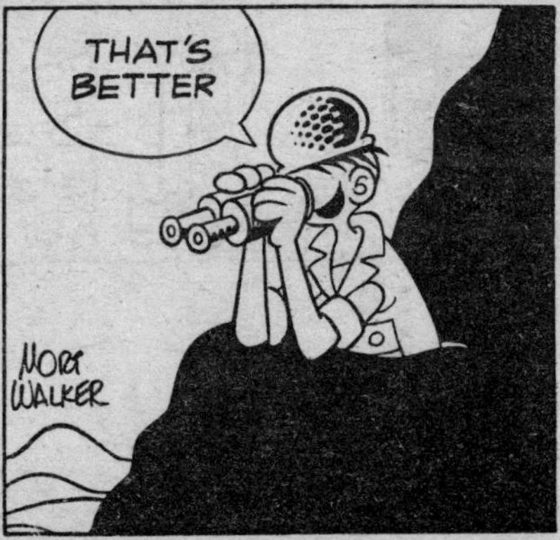
THAT'S BETTER
MORT WALKER

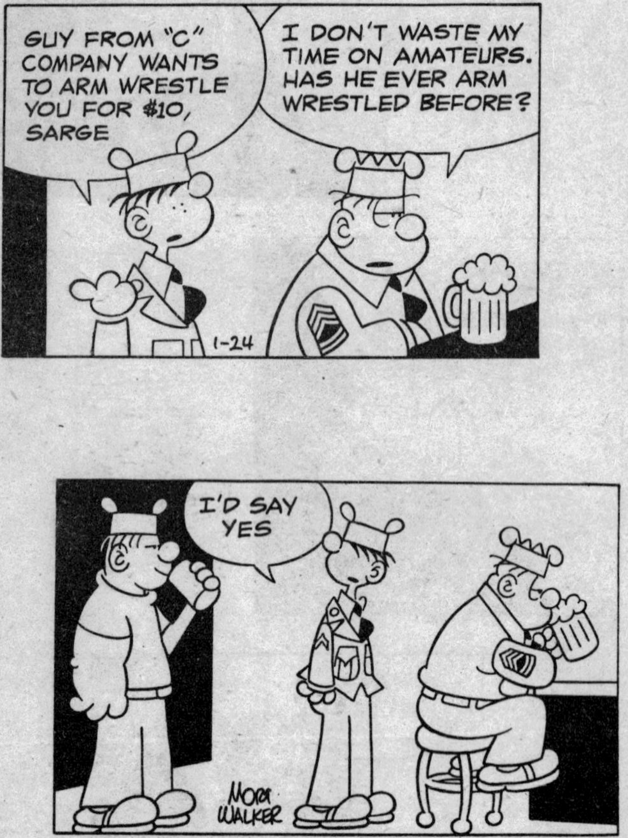
GUY FROM "C" COMPANY WANTS TO ARM WRESTLE YOU FOR $10, SARGE
I DON'T WASTE MY TIME ON AMATEURS. HAS HE EVER ARM WRESTLED BEFORE?
1-24
I'D SAY YES
MORT WALKER

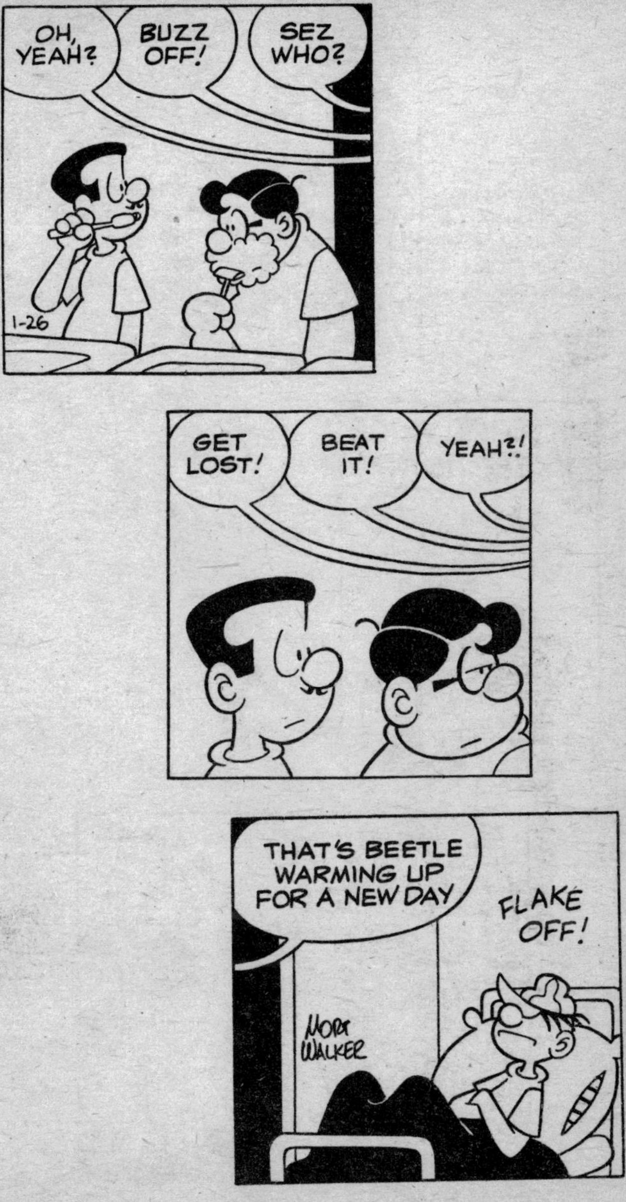
OH, YEAH?
BUZZ OFF!
SEZ WHO?
1-26
GET LOST!
BEAT IT!
YEAH?!
THAT'S BEETLE WARMING UP FOR A NEW DAY
FLAKE OFF!
MORT WALKER

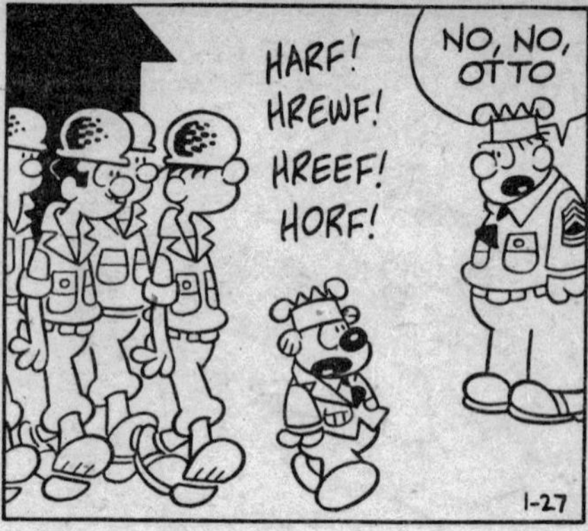
HARF! HREWF! HREEF! HORF!
NO, NO, OTTO
1-27

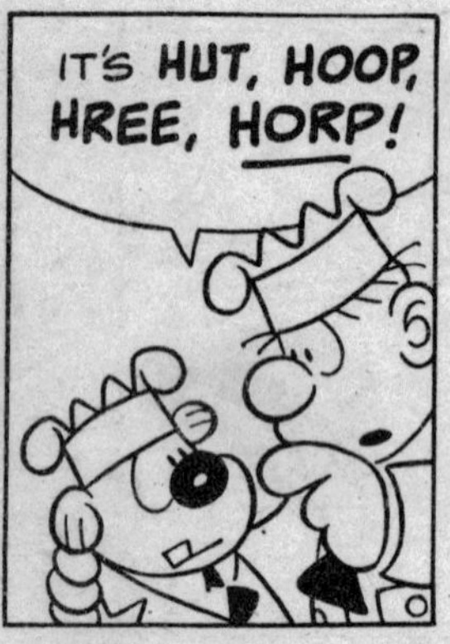
IT'S HUT, HOOP, HREE, HORP!

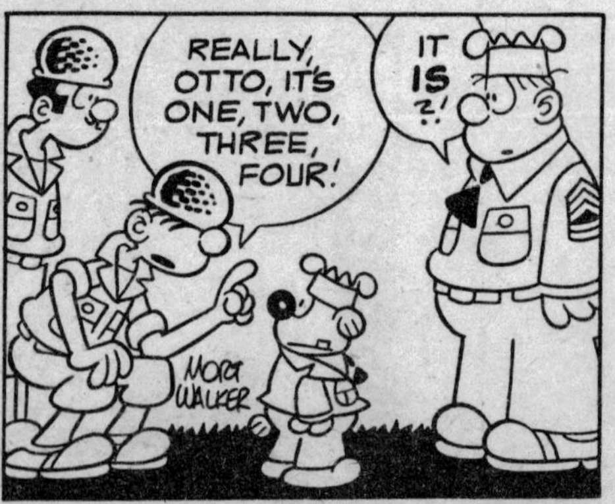
REALLY, OTTO, IT'S ONE, TWO, THREE, FOUR!
IT IS ?!
MORT WALKER

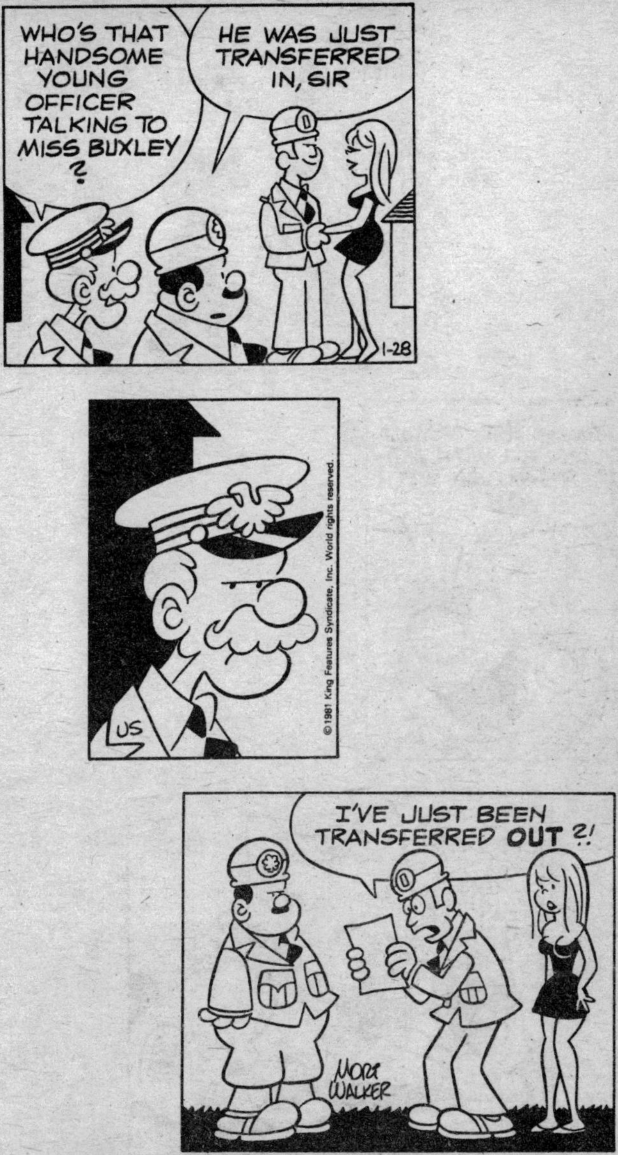
WHO'S THAT HANDSOME YOUNG OFFICER TALKING TO MISS BUXLEY ?
HE WAS JUST TRANSFERRED IN, SIR
1-28
US
© 1981 King Features Syndicate, Inc. World rights reserved.
I'VE JUST BEEN TRANSFERRED OUT ?!
MORT WALKER

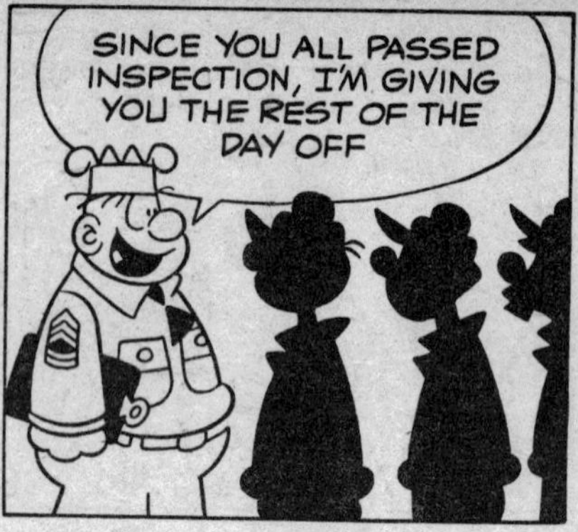
SINCE YOU ALL PASSED INSPECTION, I'M GIVING YOU THE REST OF THE DAY OFF

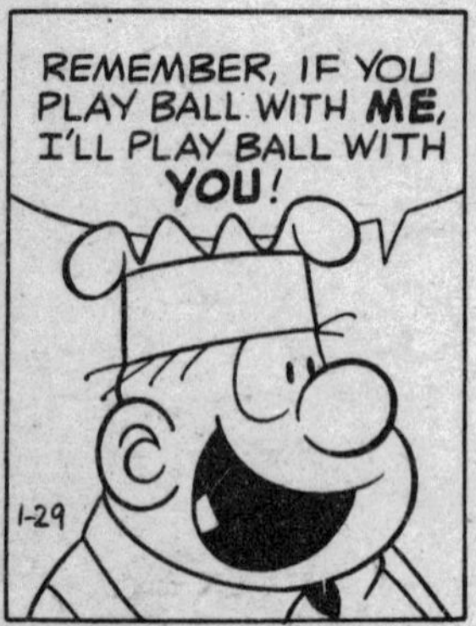
REMEMBER, IF YOU PLAY BALL WITH **ME**, I'LL PLAY BALL WITH **YOU**!
1-29

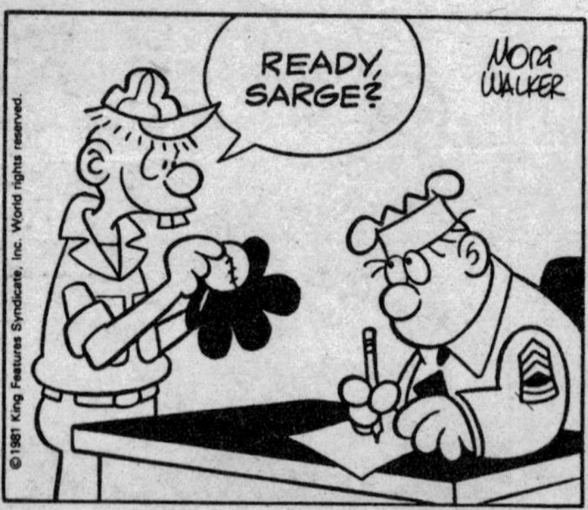
READY, SARGE?
MORT WALKER
© 1981 King Features Syndicate, Inc. World rights reserved.

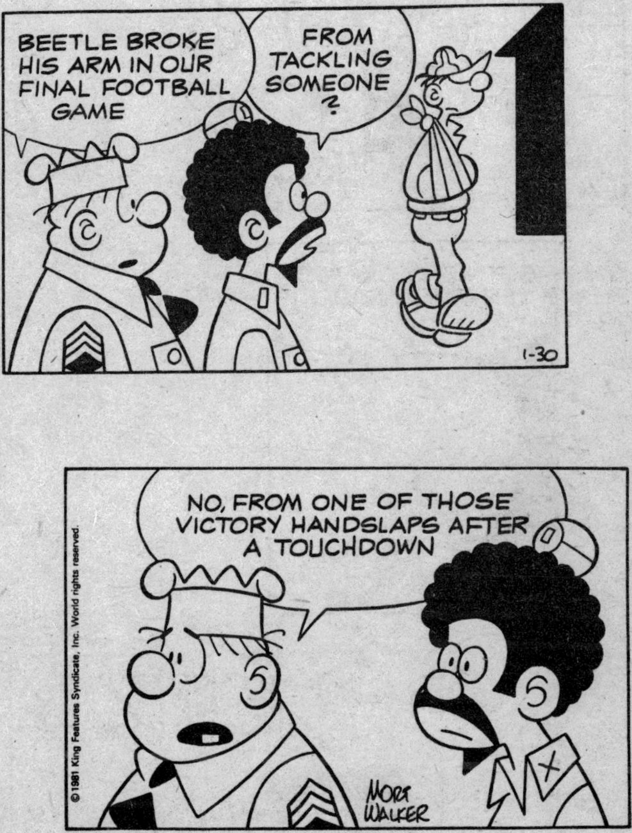
BEETLE BROKE HIS ARM IN OUR FINAL FOOTBALL GAME
FROM TACKLING SOMEONE?
1-30
NO, FROM ONE OF THOSE VICTORY HANDSLAPS AFTER A TOUCHDOWN
MORT WALKER

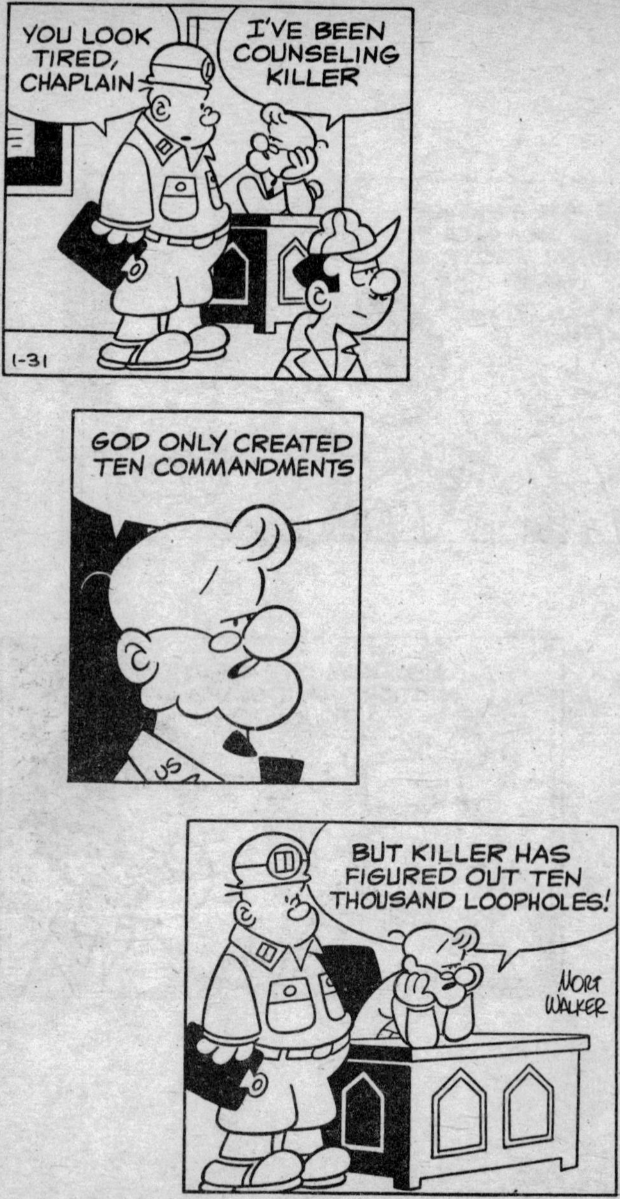
YOU LOOK TIRED, CHAPLAIN
I'VE BEEN COUNSELING KILLER
1-31
GOD ONLY CREATED TEN COMMANDMENTS
US
BUT KILLER HAS FIGURED OUT TEN THOUSAND LOOPHOLES!
MORT WALKER

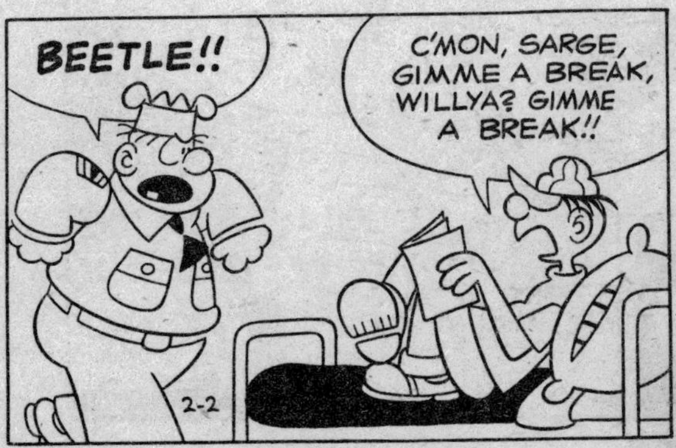
BEETLE!!
C'MON, SARGE, GIMME A BREAK, WILLYA? GIMME A BREAK!!
2-2

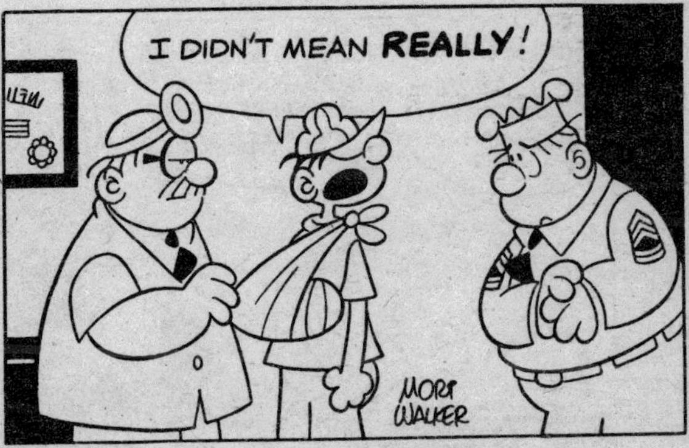
I DIDN'T MEAN **REALLY**!
MORT WALKER

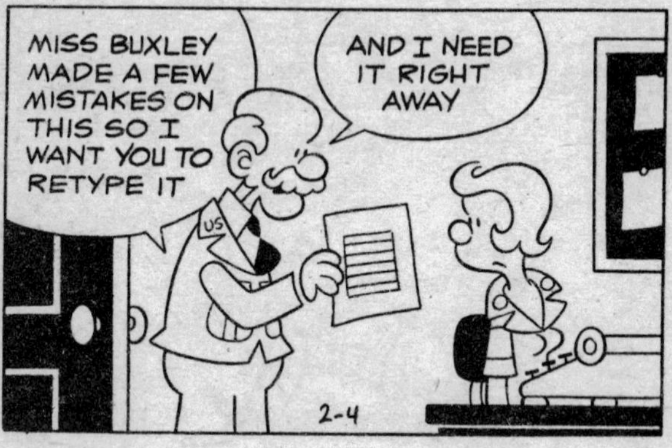
MISS BUXLEY MADE A FEW MISTAKES ON THIS SO I WANT YOU TO RETYPE IT
AND I NEED IT RIGHT AWAY
US
2-4

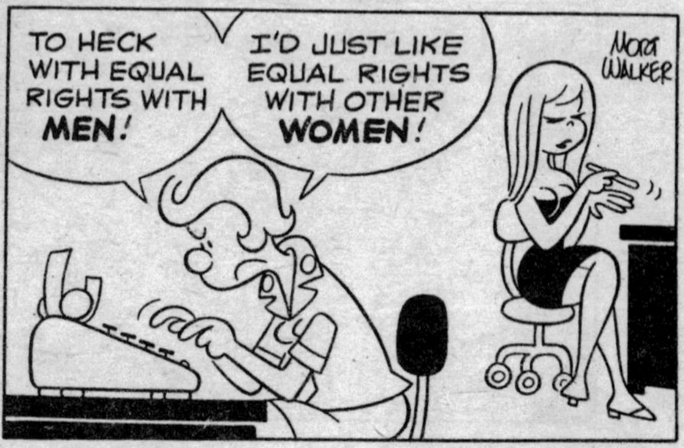
TO HECK WITH EQUAL RIGHTS WITH **MEN**!
I'D JUST LIKE EQUAL RIGHTS WITH OTHER **WOMEN**!
Mort WALKER

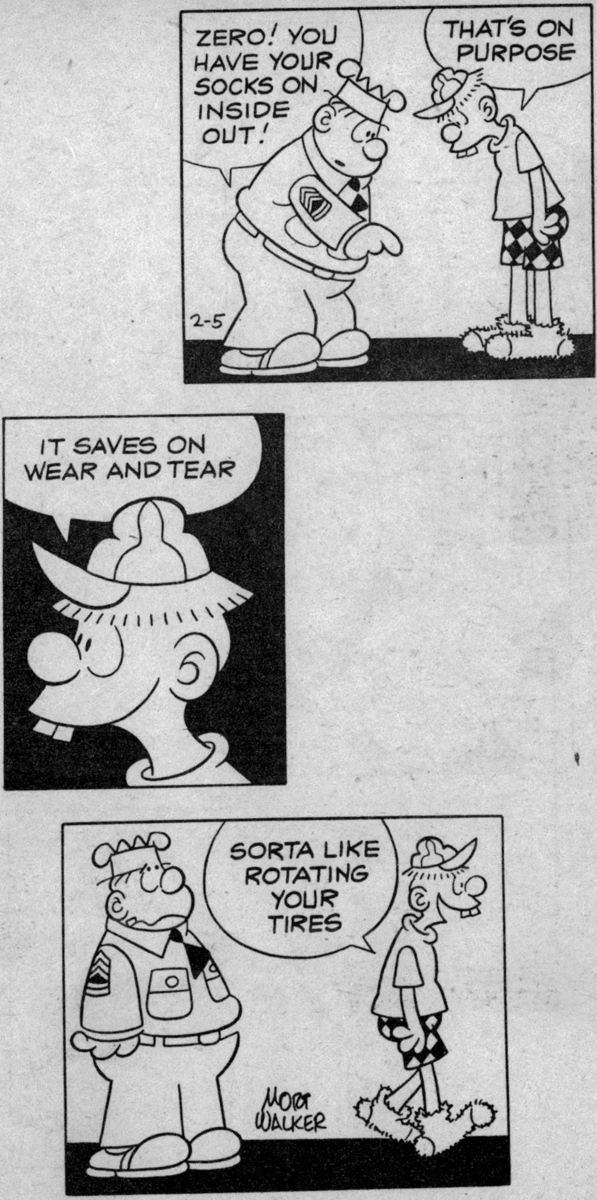
ZERO! YOU HAVE YOUR SOCKS ON INSIDE OUT!
THAT'S ON PURPOSE
2-5
IT SAVES ON WEAR AND TEAR
SORTA LIKE ROTATING YOUR TIRES
MORT WALKER

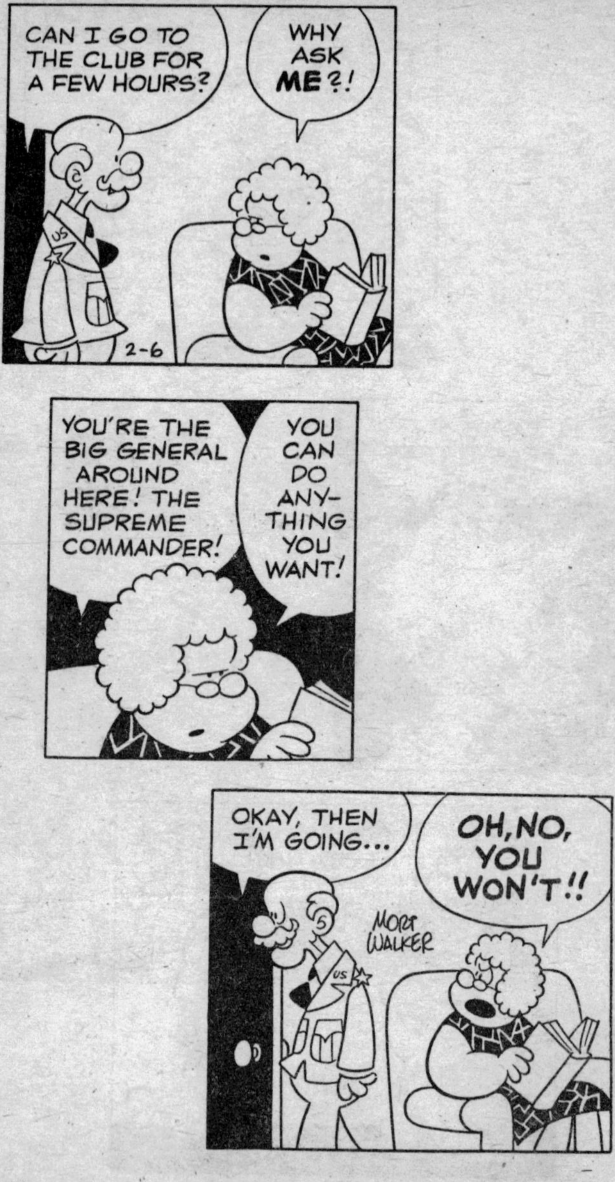
CAN I GO TO THE CLUB FOR A FEW HOURS?
WHY ASK ME?!
2-6
YOU'RE THE BIG GENERAL AROUND HERE! THE SUPREME COMMANDER!
YOU CAN DO ANY-THING YOU WANT!
OKAY, THEN I'M GOING...
OH, NO, YOU WON'T!!
MORT WALKER

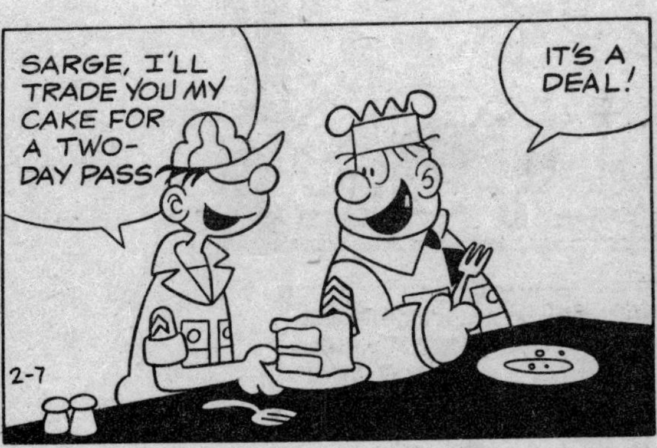
SARGE, I'LL TRADE YOU MY CAKE FOR A TWO-DAY PASS
IT'S A DEAL!
2-7

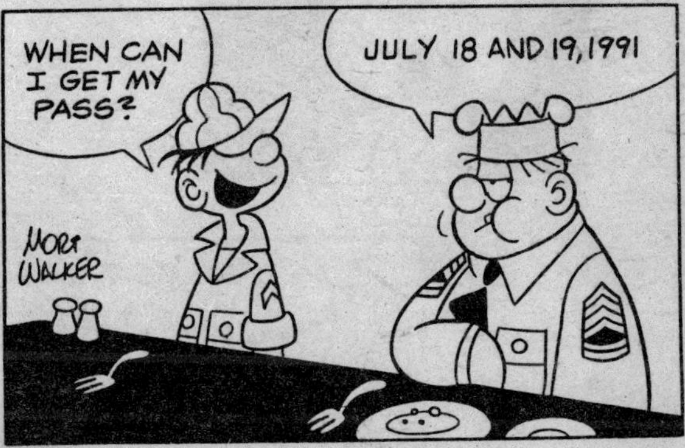
WHEN CAN I GET MY PASS?
JULY 18 AND 19, 1991
MORT WALKER

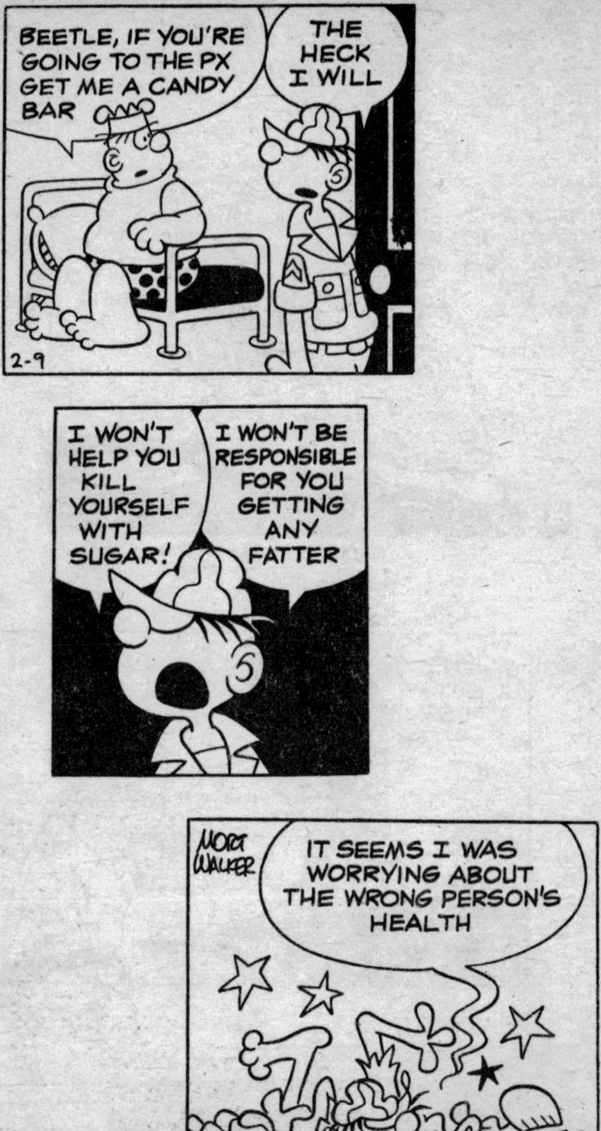
BEETLE, IF YOU'RE GOING TO THE PX GET ME A CANDY BAR
THE HECK I WILL
2-9
I WON'T HELP YOU KILL YOURSELF WITH SUGAR!
I WON'T BE RESPONSIBLE FOR YOU GETTING ANY FATTER
MORT WALKER
IT SEEMS I WAS WORRYING ABOUT THE WRONG PERSON'S HEALTH

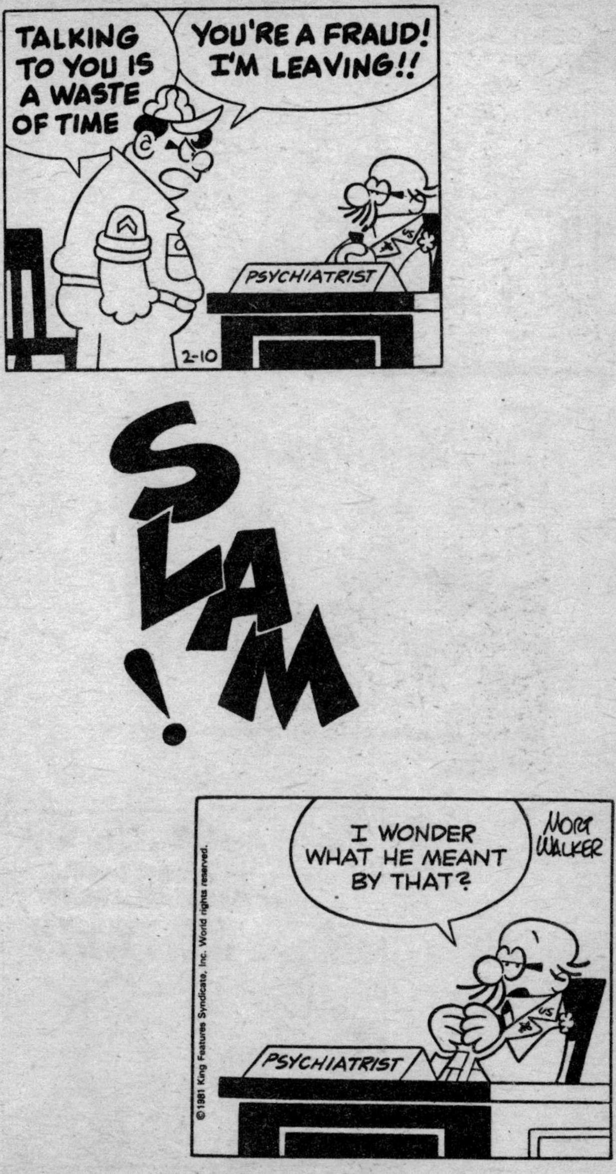
TALKING TO YOU IS A WASTE OF TIME
YOU'RE A FRAUD! I'M LEAVING!!
PSYCHIATRIST
2-10
SLAM!
I WONDER WHAT HE MEANT BY THAT?
MORT WALKER
PSYCHIATRIST
© 1981 King Features Syndicate, Inc. World rights reserved.

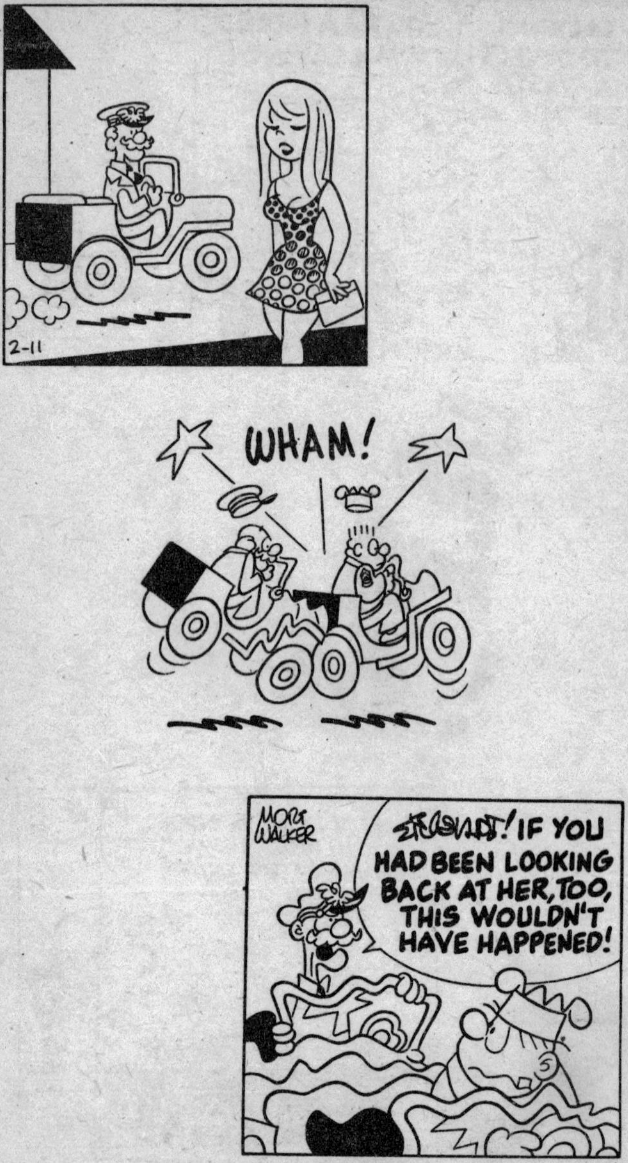
2-11
WHAM!
MORT WALKER
! IF YOU HAD BEEN LOOKING BACK AT HER, TOO, THIS WOULDN'T HAVE HAPPENED!

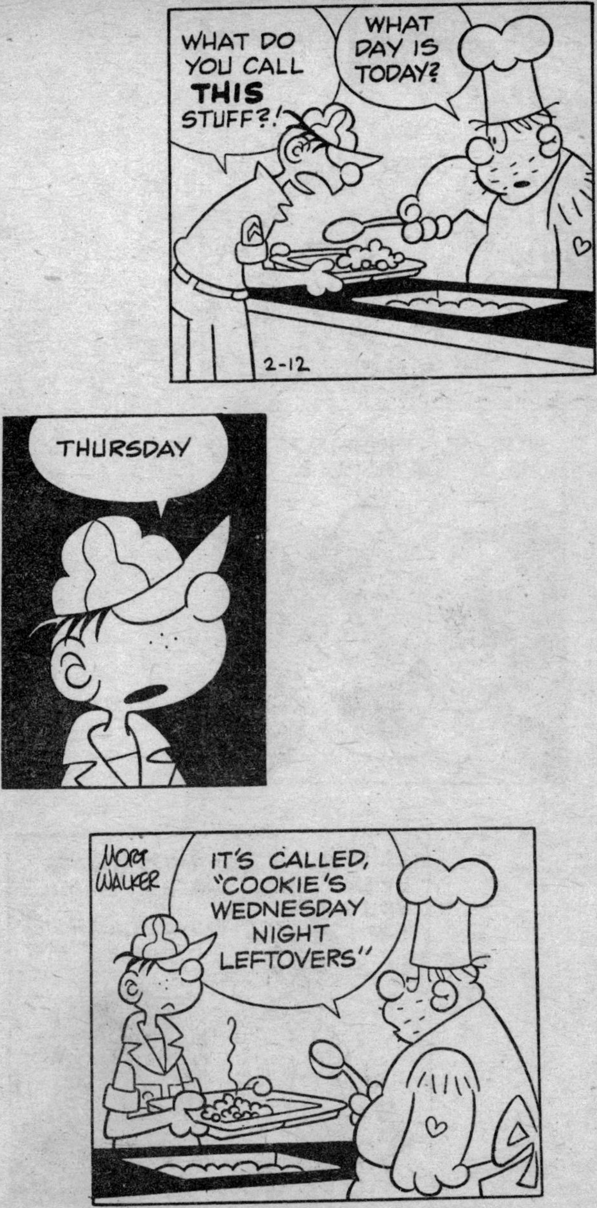
WHAT DO YOU CALL **THIS** STUFF?!
WHAT DAY IS TODAY?
2-12
THURSDAY
MORT WALKER
IT'S CALLED, "COOKIE'S WEDNESDAY NIGHT LEFTOVERS"

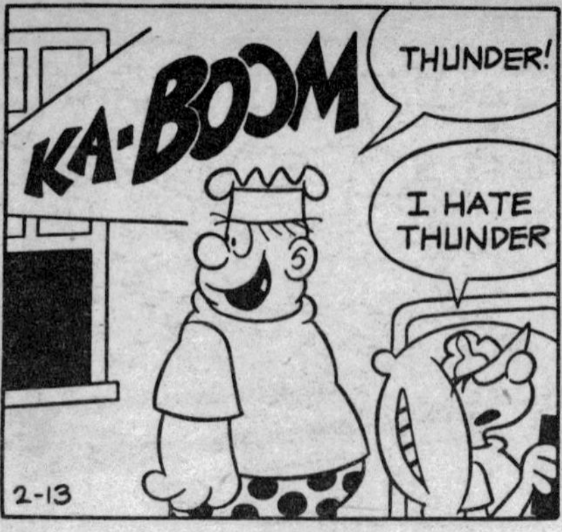
KA-BOOM
THUNDER!
I HATE THUNDER
2-13

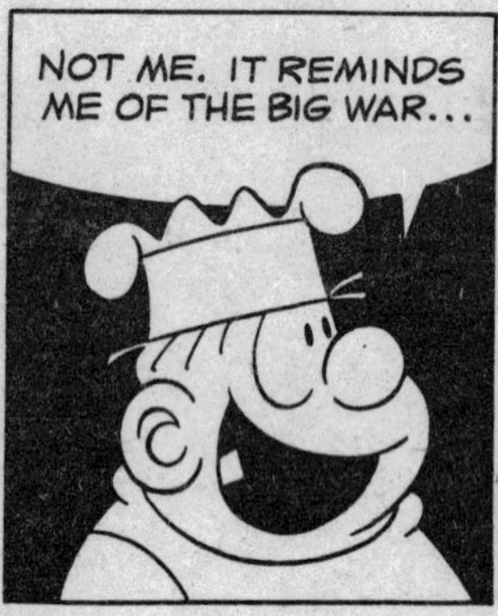
NOT ME. IT REMINDS ME OF THE BIG WAR...

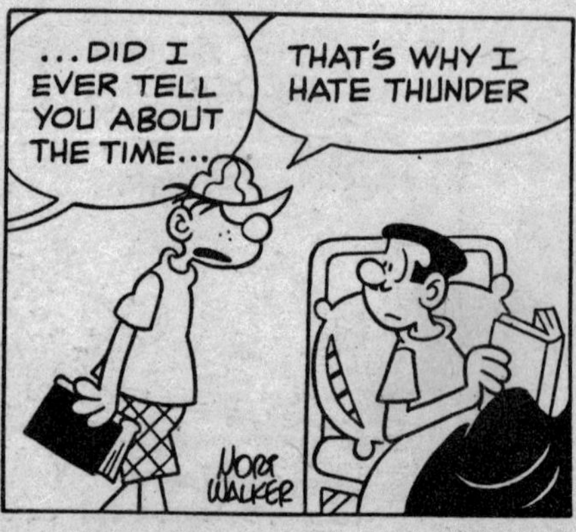
THAT'S WHY I HATE THUNDER
...DID I EVER TELL YOU ABOUT THE TIME...
MORT WALKER

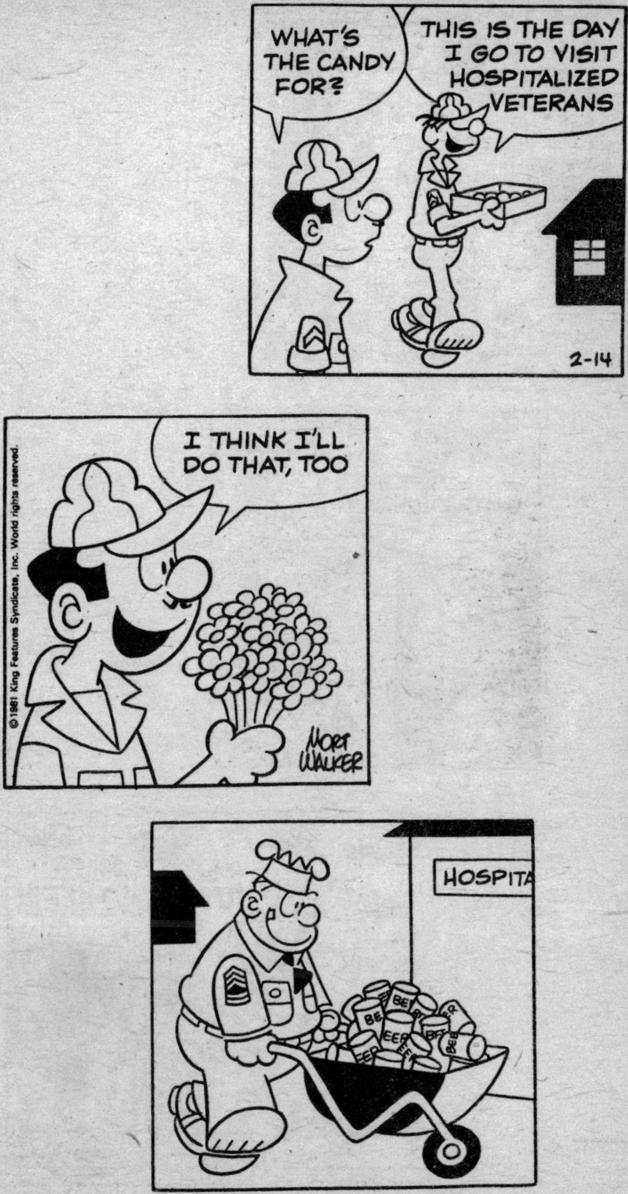
WHAT'S THE CANDY FOR?
THIS IS THE DAY I GO TO VISIT HOSPITALIZED VETERANS
2-14
I THINK I'LL DO THAT, TOO
© 1981 King Features Syndicate, Inc. World rights reserved.
MORT WALKER
HOSPITA

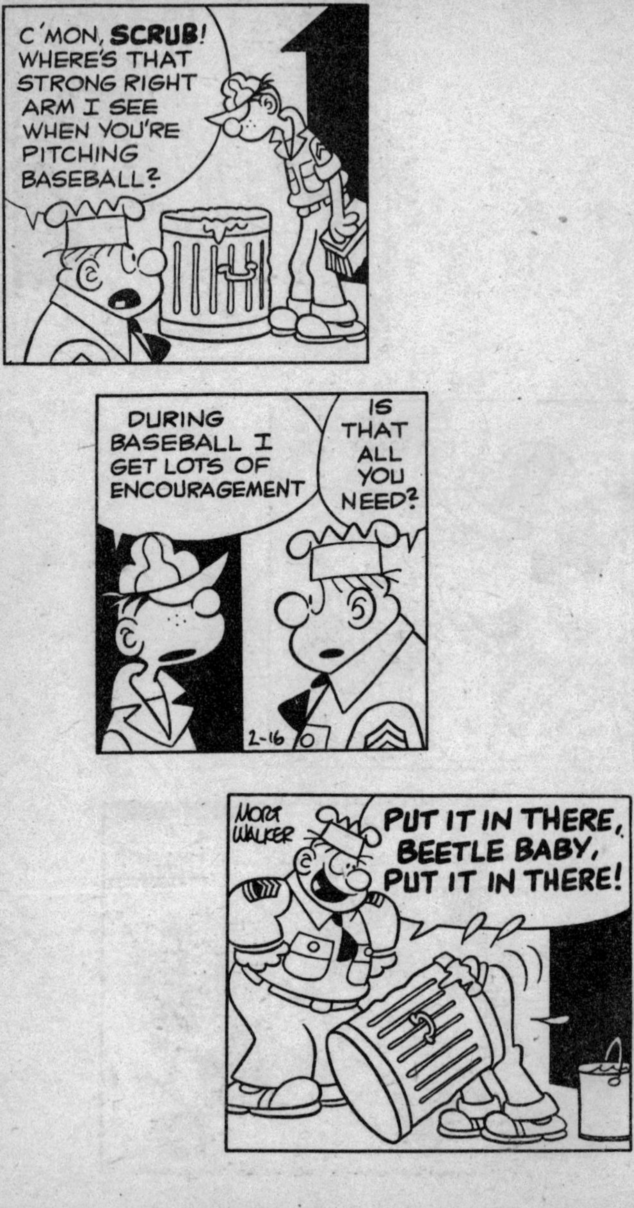
C'MON, **SCRUB**! WHERE'S THAT STRONG RIGHT ARM I SEE WHEN YOU'RE PITCHING BASEBALL?
DURING BASEBALL I GET LOTS OF ENCOURAGEMENT
IS THAT ALL YOU NEED?
2-16
MORT WALKER
PUT IT IN THERE, BEETLE BABY, PUT IT IN THERE!

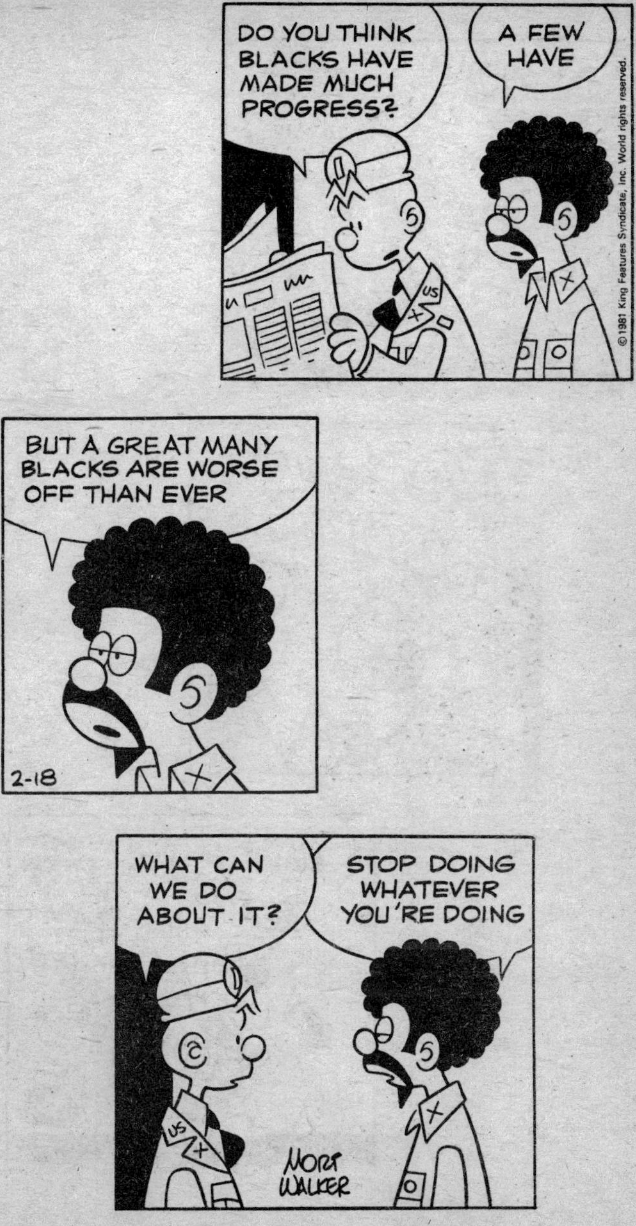
DO YOU THINK BLACKS HAVE MADE MUCH PROGRESS?
A FEW HAVE
©1981 King Features Syndicate, Inc. World rights reserved.
BUT A GREAT MANY BLACKS ARE WORSE OFF THAN EVER
2-18
WHAT CAN WE DO ABOUT IT?
STOP DOING WHATEVER YOU'RE DOING
MORT WALKER

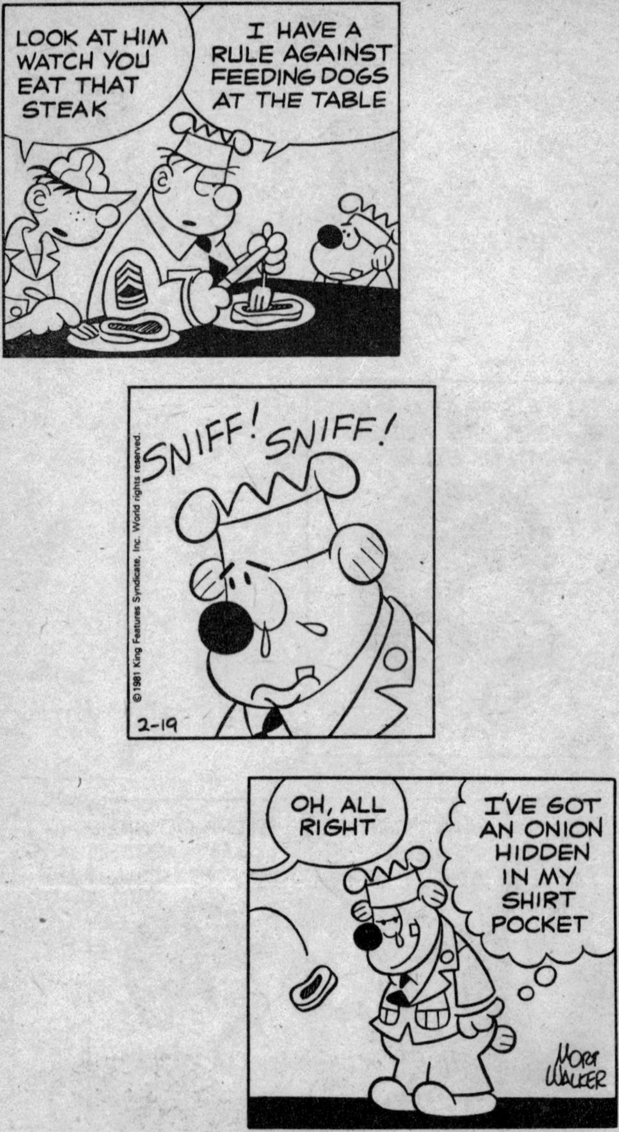
LOOK AT HIM WATCH YOU EAT THAT STEAK
I HAVE A RULE AGAINST FEEDING DOGS AT THE TABLE
SNIFF! SNIFF!
© 1981 King Features Syndicate, Inc. World rights reserved.
2-19
OH, ALL RIGHT
I'VE GOT AN ONION HIDDEN IN MY SHIRT POCKET
MORT WALKER

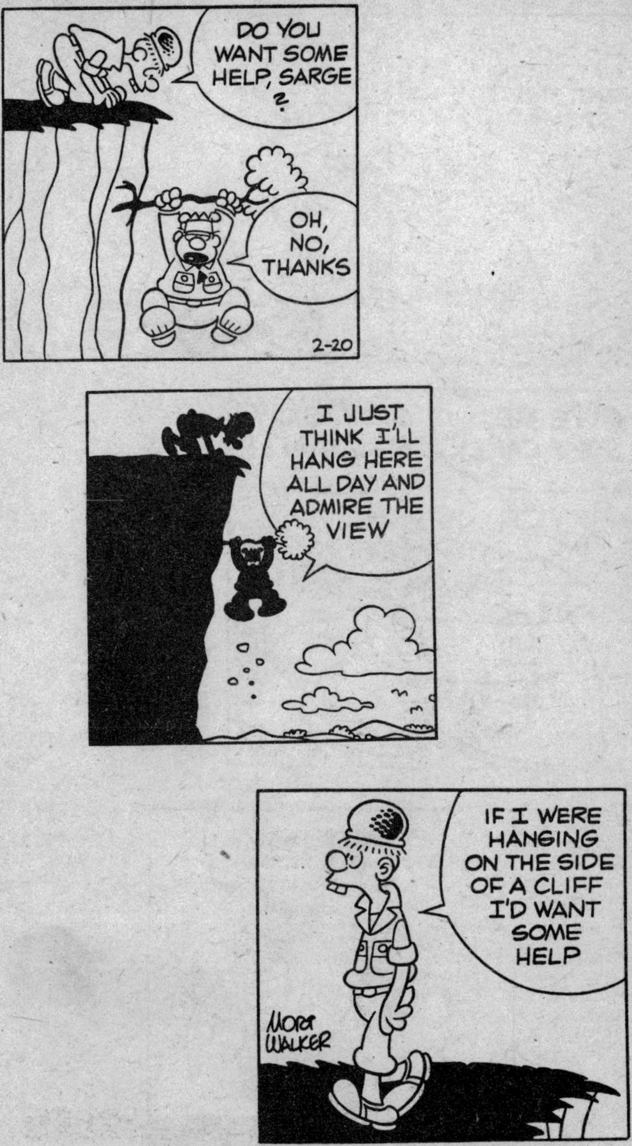
DO YOU WANT SOME HELP, SARGE?
OH, NO, THANKS
2-20
I JUST THINK I'LL HANG HERE ALL DAY AND ADMIRE THE VIEW
IF I WERE HANGING ON THE SIDE OF A CLIFF I'D WANT SOME HELP
MORT WALKER

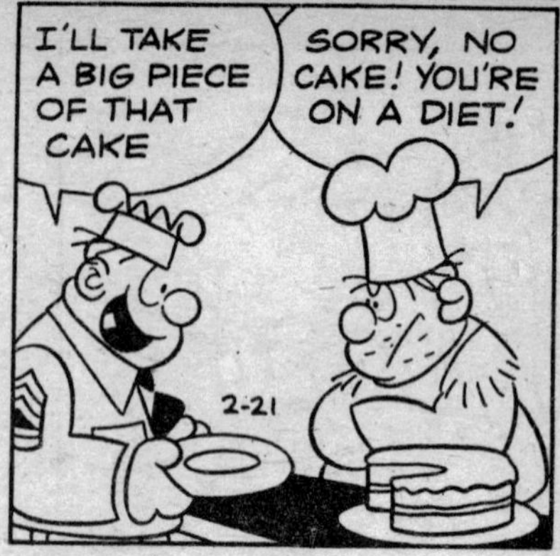
I'LL TAKE A BIG PIECE OF THAT CAKE
SORRY, NO CAKE! YOU'RE ON A DIET!
2-21

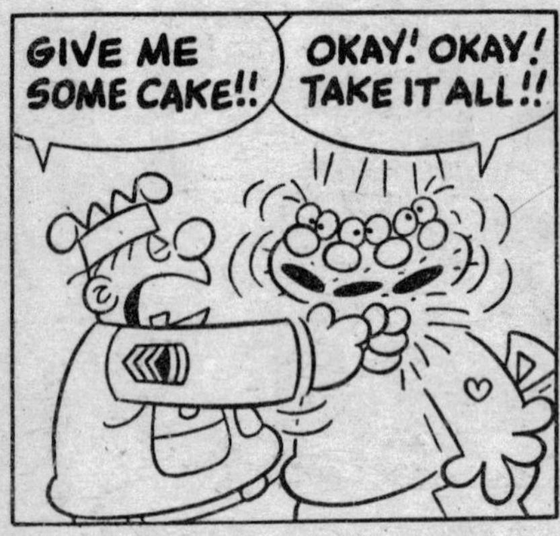
GIVE ME SOME CAKE!!
OKAY! OKAY! TAKE IT ALL!!

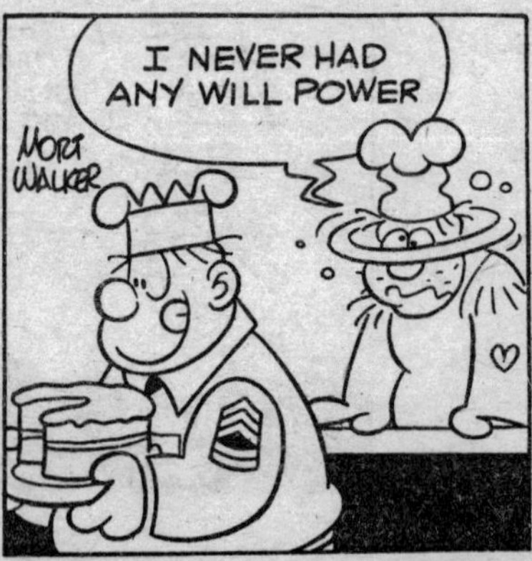
I NEVER HAD ANY WILL POWER
MORT WALKER

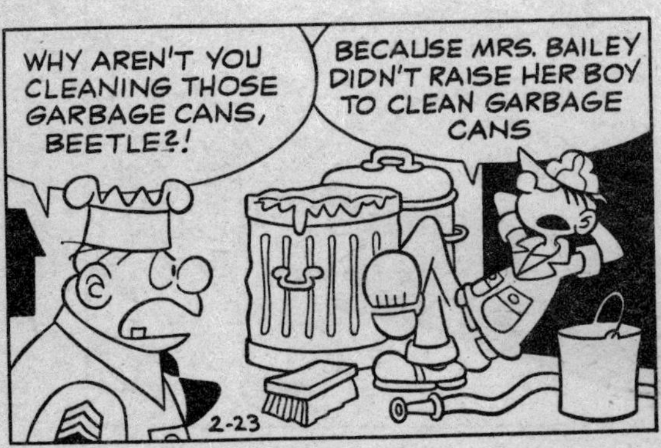
WHY AREN'T YOU CLEANING THOSE GARBAGE CANS, BEETLE?!
BECAUSE MRS. BAILEY DIDN'T RAISE HER BOY TO CLEAN GARBAGE CANS
2-23

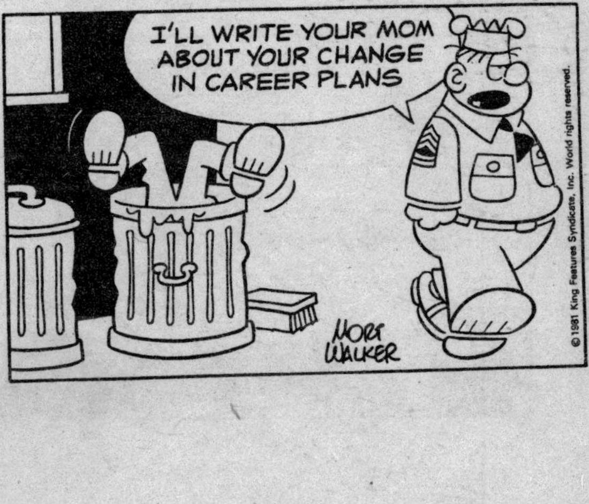
I'LL WRITE YOUR MOM ABOUT YOUR CHANGE IN CAREER PLANS
MORT WALKER
© 1981 King Features Syndicate, Inc. World rights reserved.

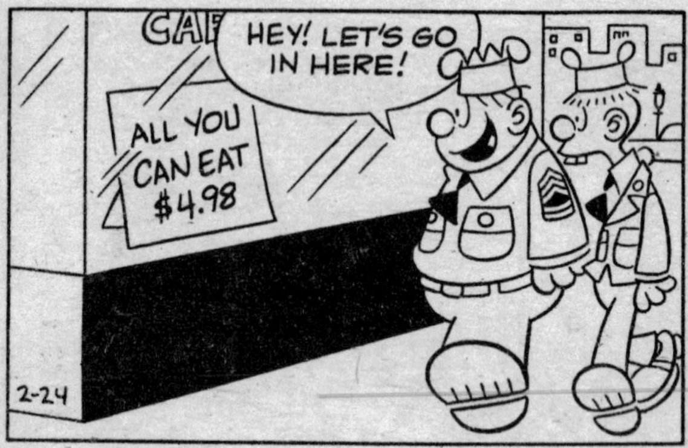
CAF
HEY! LET'S GO IN HERE!
ALL YOU CAN EAT $4.98
2-24

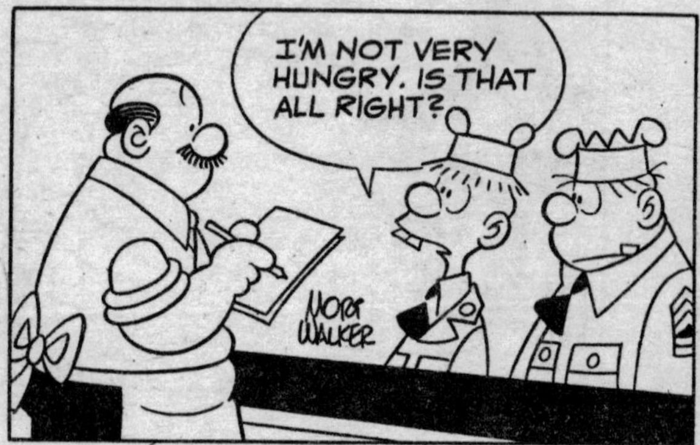
I'M NOT VERY HUNGRY. IS THAT ALL RIGHT?
MORT WALKER

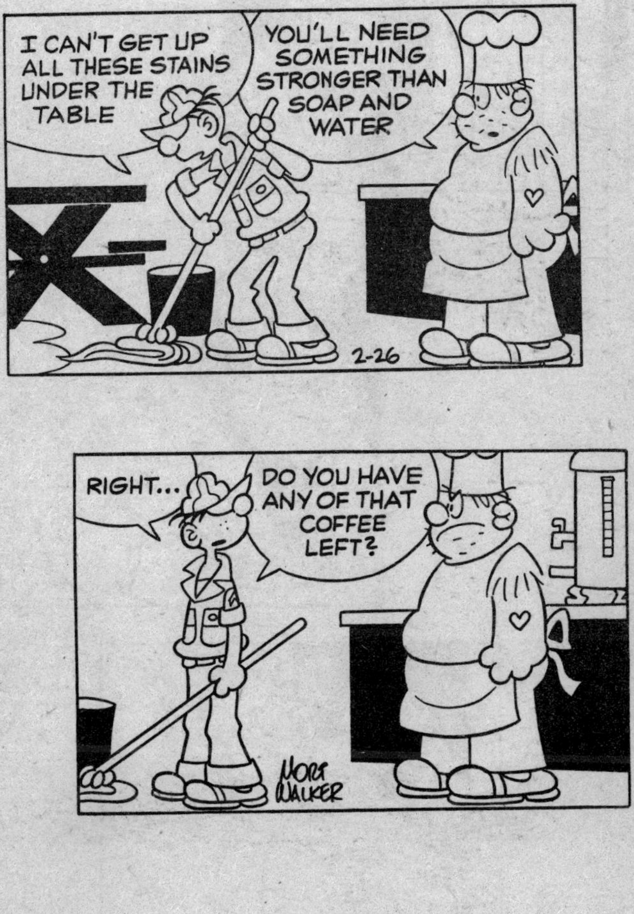
I CAN'T GET UP ALL THESE STAINS UNDER THE TABLE
YOU'LL NEED SOMETHING STRONGER THAN SOAP AND WATER
2-26
RIGHT...
DO YOU HAVE ANY OF THAT COFFEE LEFT?
MORT WALKER

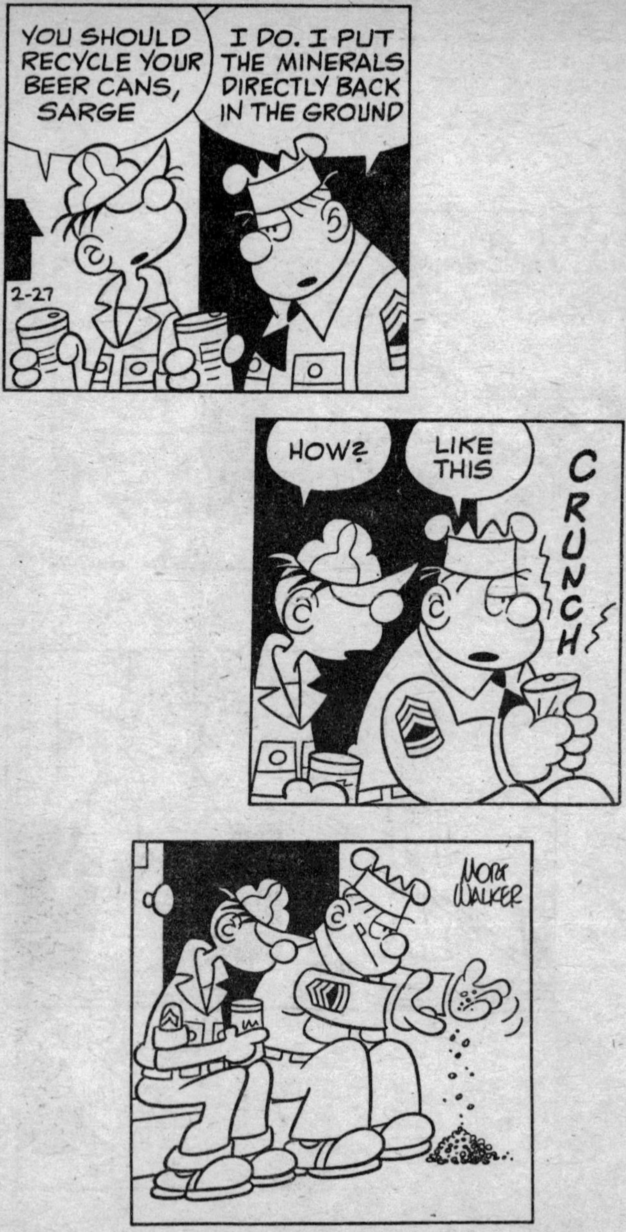
YOU SHOULD RECYCLE YOUR BEER CANS, SARGE
I DO. I PUT THE MINERALS DIRECTLY BACK IN THE GROUND
2-27
HOW?
LIKE THIS
CRUNCH
MORT WALKER

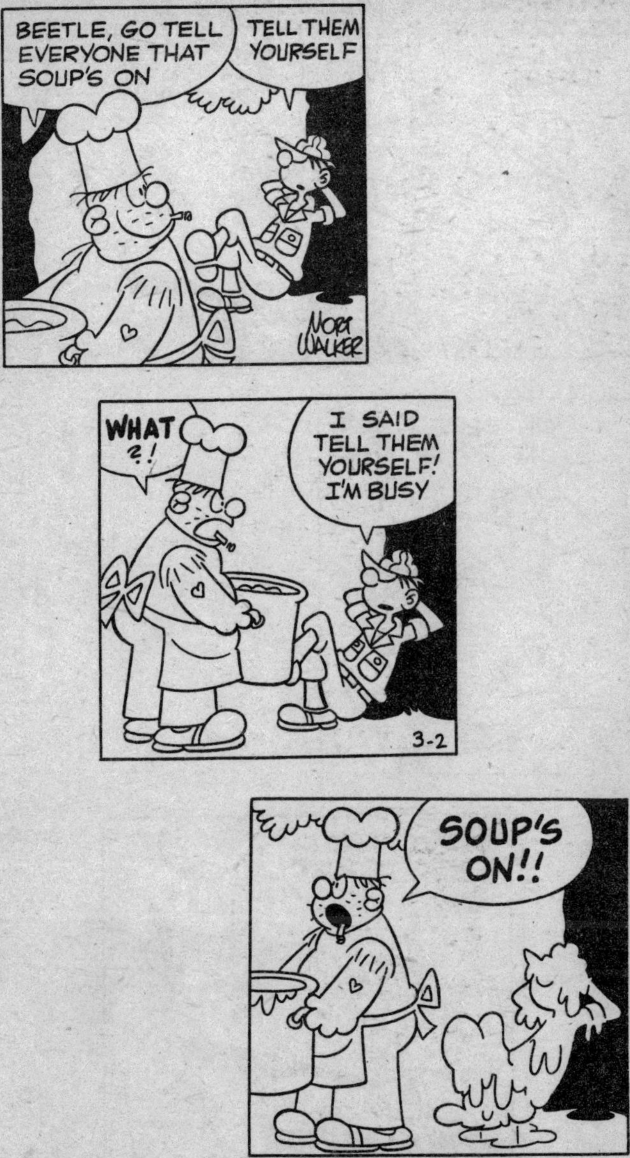

BEETLE, GO TELL EVERYONE THAT SOUP'S ON
TELL THEM YOURSELF
MORT WALKER
WHAT ?!
I SAID TELL THEM YOURSELF! I'M BUSY
3-2
SOUP'S ON!!

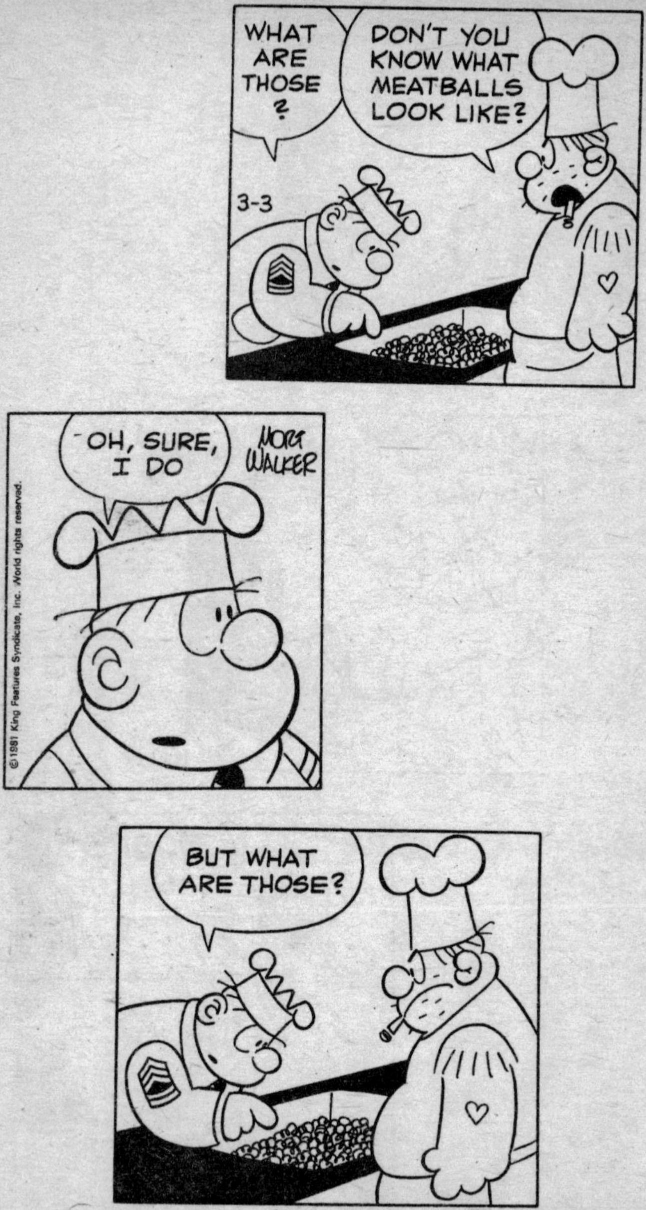
WHAT ARE THOSE?
DON'T YOU KNOW WHAT MEATBALLS LOOK LIKE?
3-3
OH, SURE, I DO
MORT WALKER
©1981 King Features Syndicate, Inc. World rights reserved.
BUT WHAT ARE THOSE?

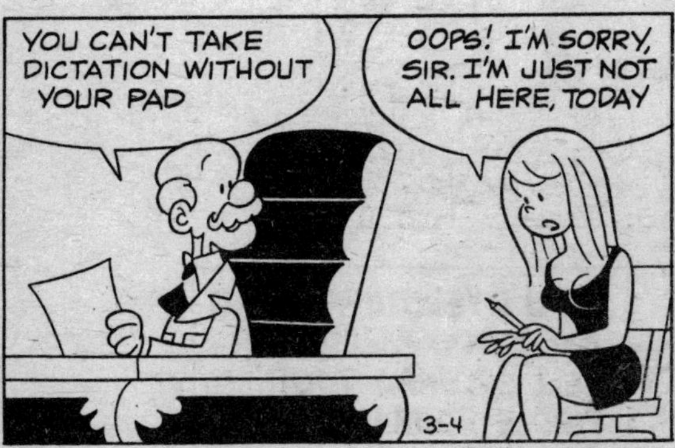
YOU CAN'T TAKE DICTATION WITHOUT YOUR PAD
OOPS! I'M SORRY, SIR. I'M JUST NOT ALL HERE, TODAY
3-4

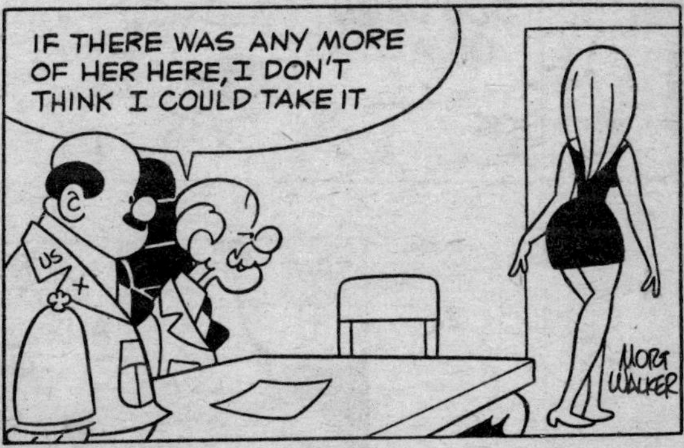
IF THERE WAS ANY MORE OF HER HERE, I DON'T THINK I COULD TAKE IT
US
MORT WALKER

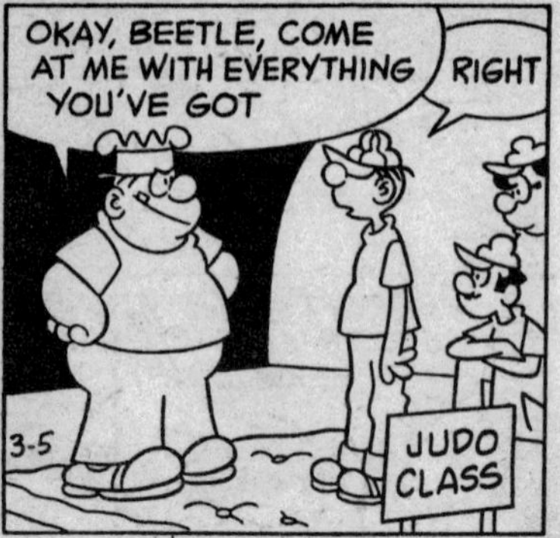
OKAY, BEETLE, COME AT ME WITH EVERYTHING YOU'VE GOT
RIGHT
3-5
JUDO CLASS

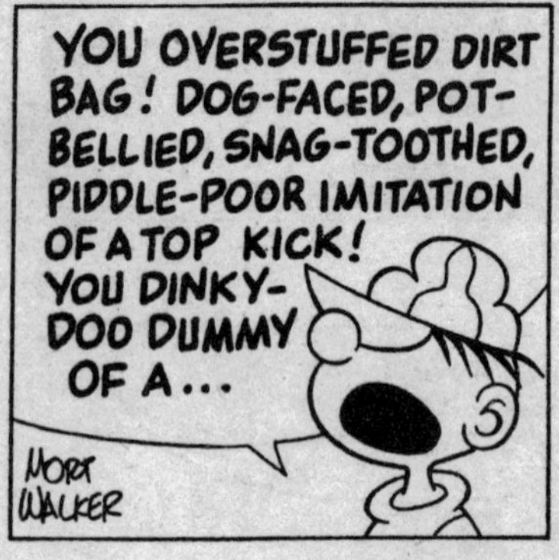
YOU OVERSTUFFED DIRT BAG! DOG-FACED, POT-BELLIED, SNAG-TOOTHED, PIDDLE-POOR IMITATION OF A TOP KICK! YOU DINKY-DOO DUMMY OF A...
MORT WALKER

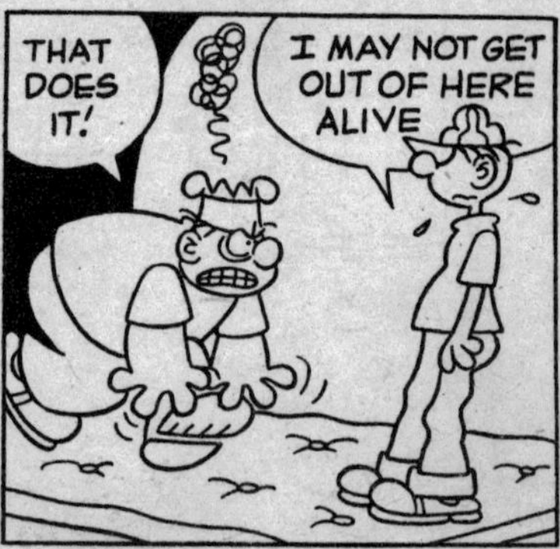
THAT DOES IT!
I MAY NOT GET OUT OF HERE ALIVE

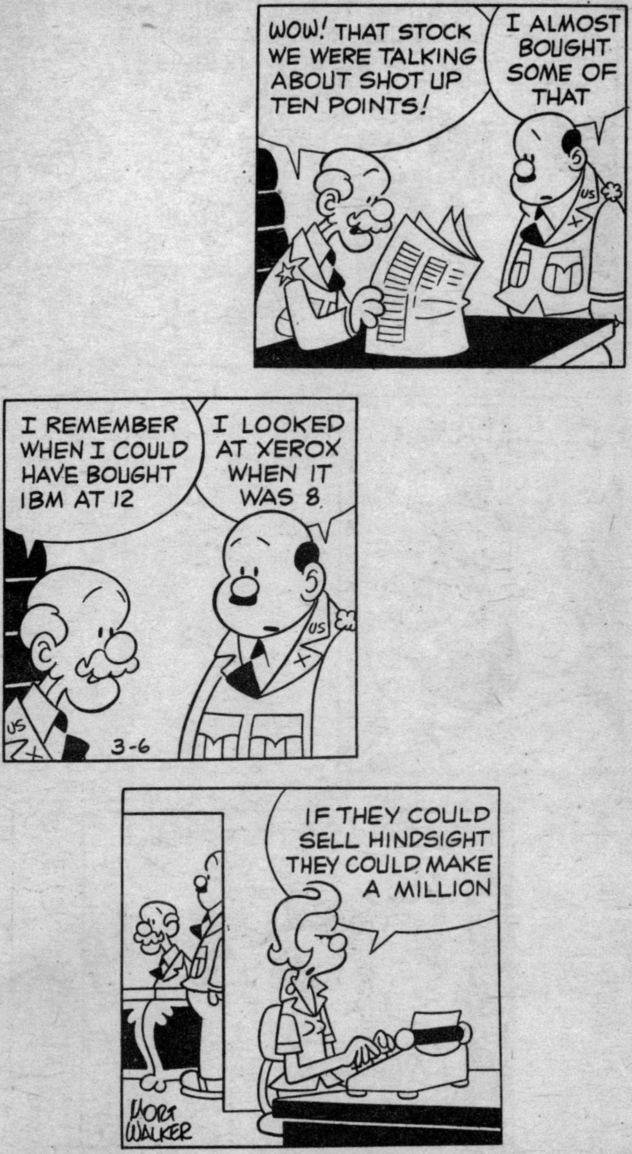
WOW! THAT STOCK WE WERE TALKING ABOUT SHOT UP TEN POINTS!
I ALMOST BOUGHT SOME OF THAT
US
I REMEMBER WHEN I COULD HAVE BOUGHT IBM AT 12
I LOOKED AT XEROX WHEN IT WAS 8
US
US
3-6
IF THEY COULD SELL HINDSIGHT THEY COULD MAKE A MILLION
MORT WALKER

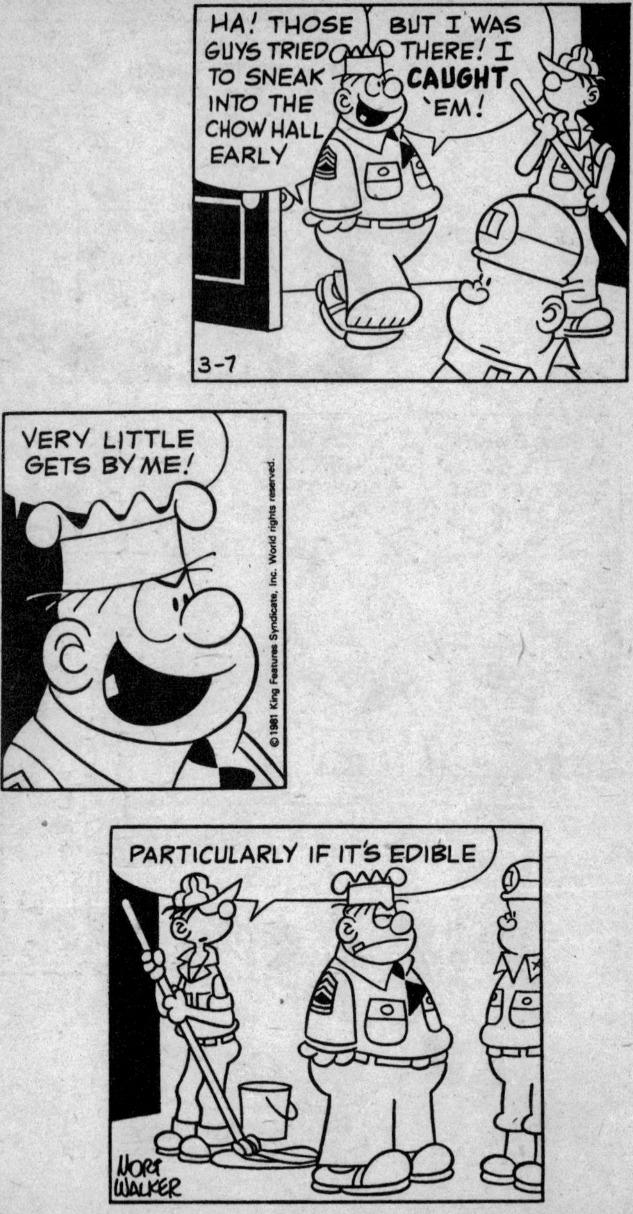
HA! THOSE GUYS TRIED TO SNEAK INTO THE CHOW HALL EARLY
BUT I WAS THERE! I CAUGHT 'EM!
3-7
VERY LITTLE GETS BY ME!
PARTICULARLY IF IT'S EDIBLE
MORT WALKER

HOW LONG HAS IT BEEN SINCE YOU WASHED YOUR SOCKS, BEETLE?
I DON'T KNOW
3-9
WHY DO YOU ASK ?
MORT WALKER
© 1981 King Features Syndicate, Inc. World rights reserved.

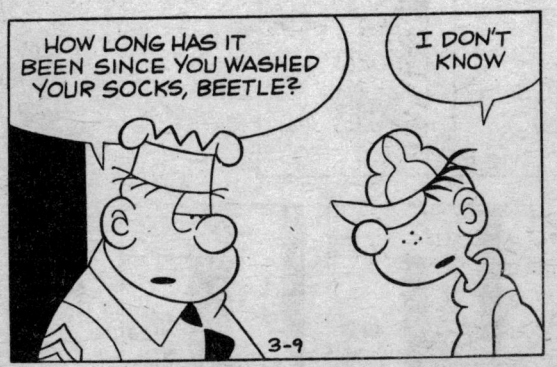

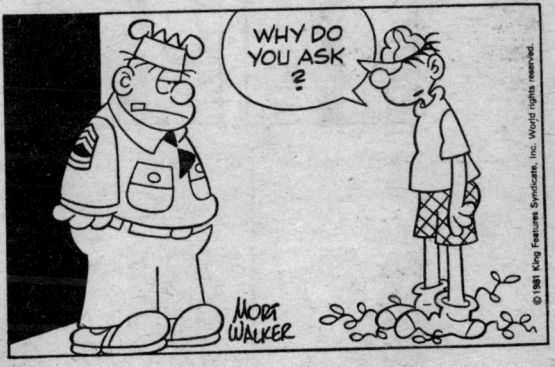

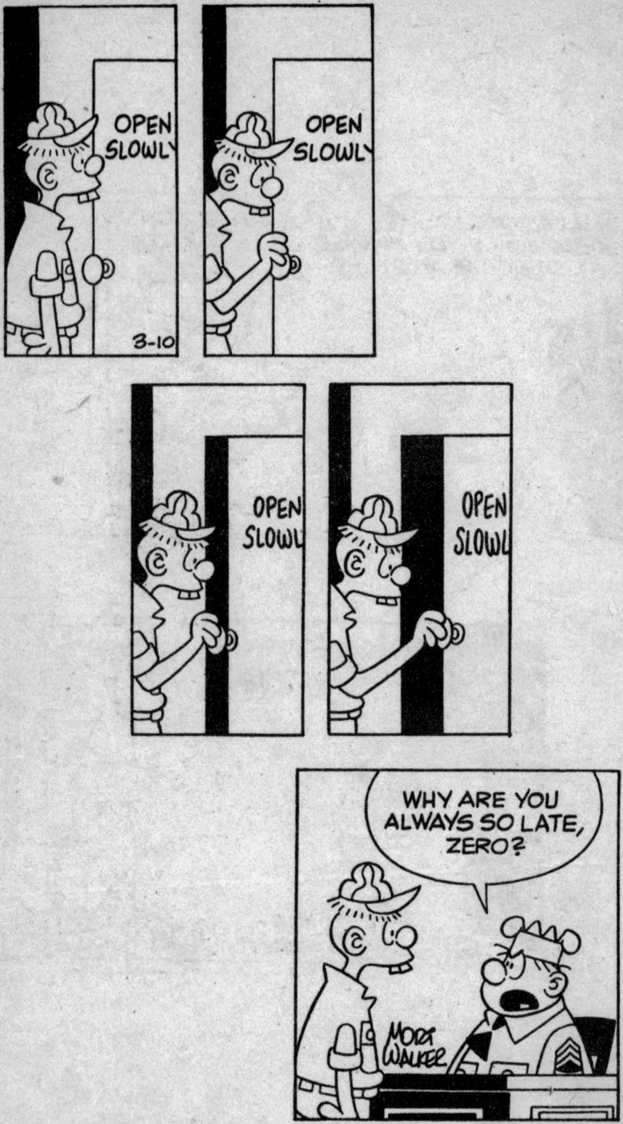
OPEN SLOWLY
3-10
OPEN SLOWLY
OPEN SLOWL
OPEN SLOWL
WHY ARE YOU ALWAYS SO LATE, ZERO?
MORT WALKER

HOW COME MISS BUXLEY GETS THE NEW TYPEWRITER?!
YOU'VE HAD MORE EXPERIENCE AND DON'T NEED ALL THE NEW FEATURES
3-11
BESIDES, BETTER EQUIPMENT RATES BETTER EQUIPMENT ...RIGHT?
♪
US
US
MORT WALKER
© 1981 King Features Syndicate, Inc. World rights reserved.

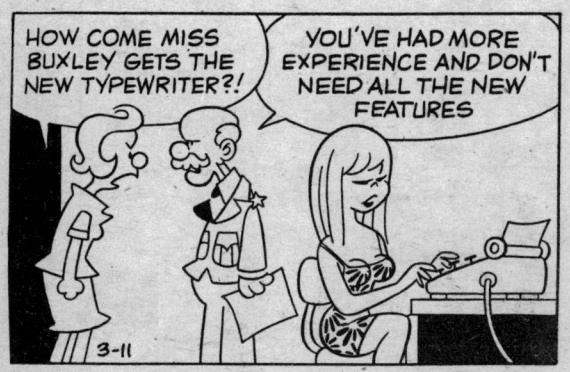

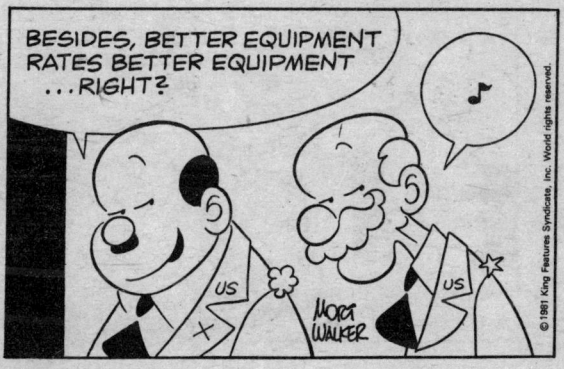

SARGE, IF OVEREATING DOESN'T KILL YOU, THE ADDITIVES WILL
HEY! I ONLY USE FRESH FOOD! THERE AREN'T ANY ADDITIVES!
MORT WALKER
I'M TALKING ABOUT THE KETCHUP, MUSTARD, SALT, PEPPER, GARLIC, SOY SAUCE, TABASCO, HORSERADISH AND CHILI POWDER!
3-12

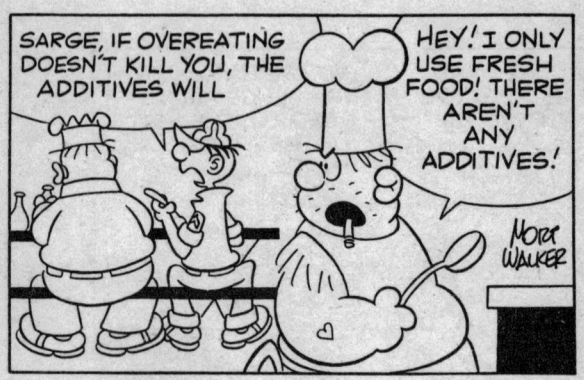

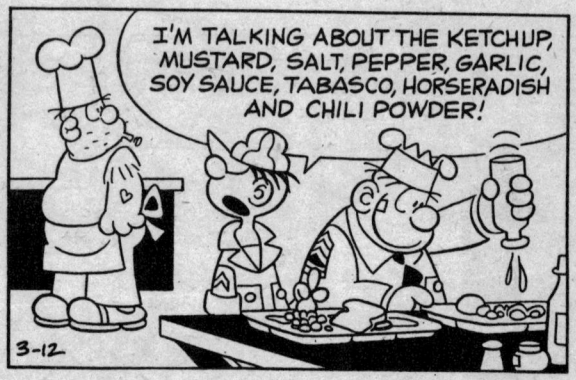

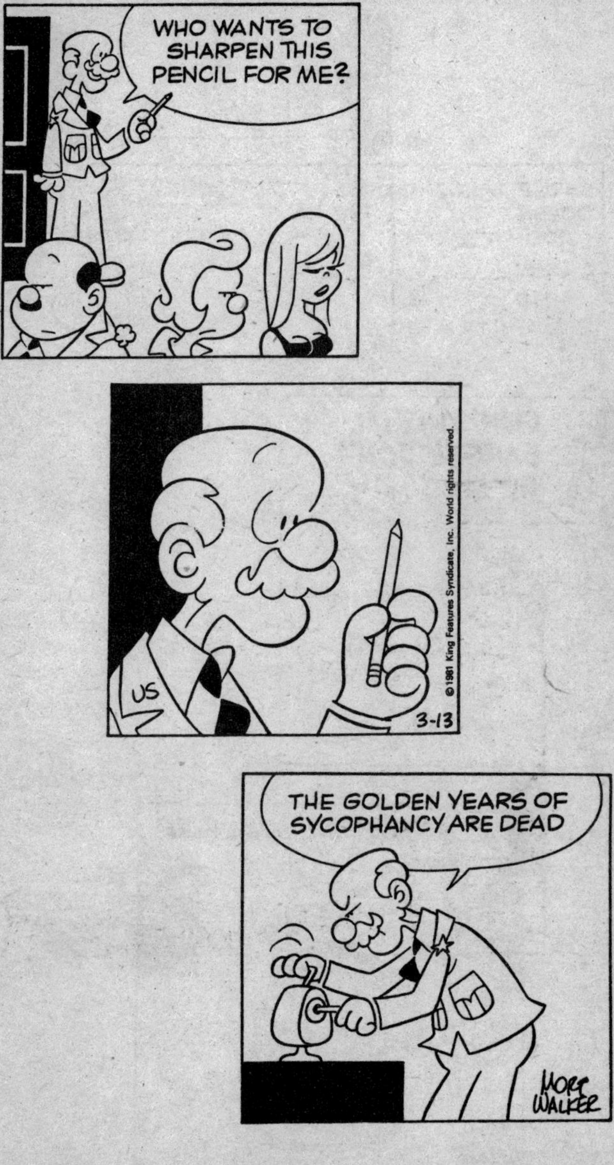
WHO WANTS TO SHARPEN THIS PENCIL FOR ME?
US
©1981 King Features Syndicate, Inc. World rights reserved.
3-13
THE GOLDEN YEARS OF SYCOPHANCY ARE DEAD
MORT WALKER

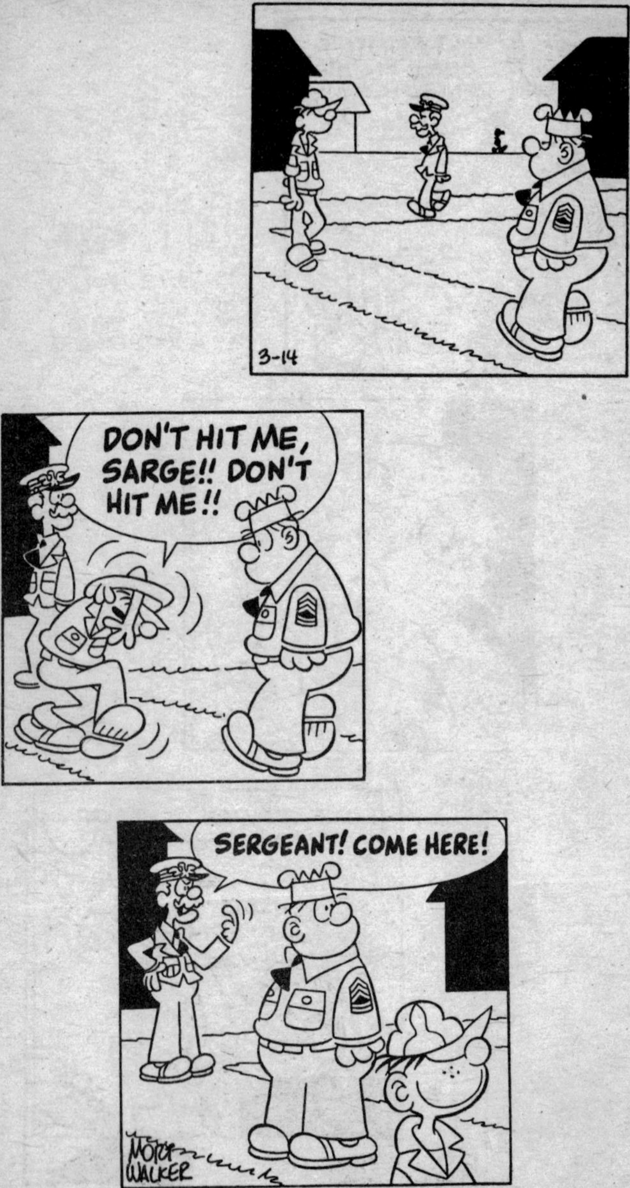
3-14
DON'T HIT ME, SARGE!! DON'T HIT ME!!
SERGEANT! COME HERE!
MORT WALKER

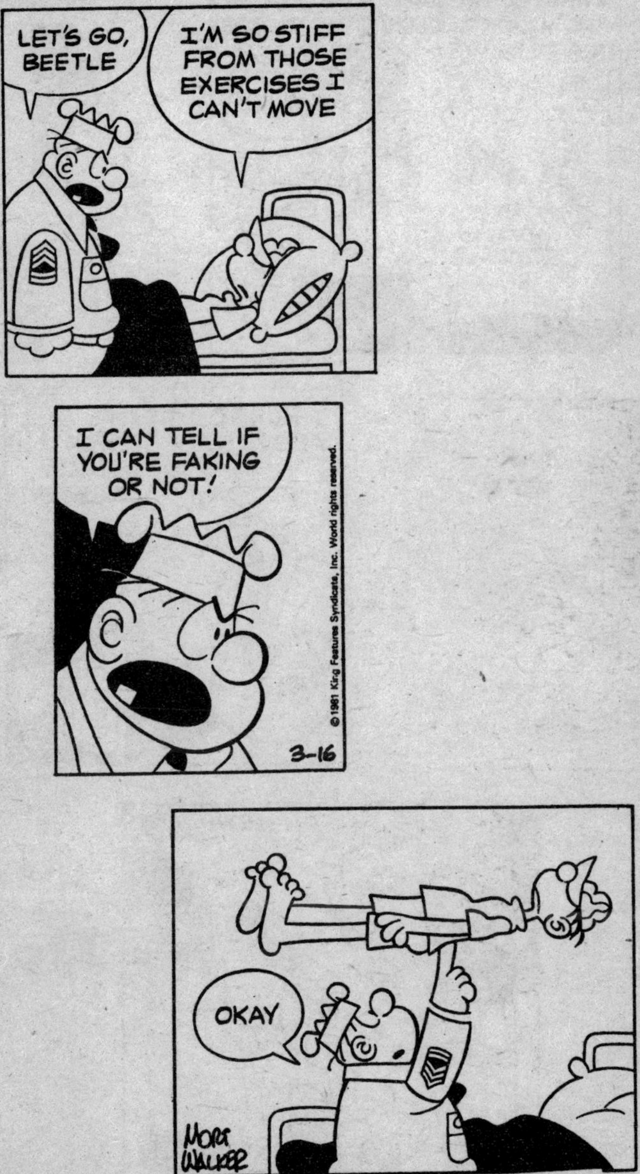
LET'S GO, BEETLE
I'M SO STIFF FROM THOSE EXERCISES I CAN'T MOVE
I CAN TELL IF YOU'RE FAKING OR NOT!
© 1981 King Features Syndicate, Inc. World rights reserved.
3-16
OKAY
MORT WALKER

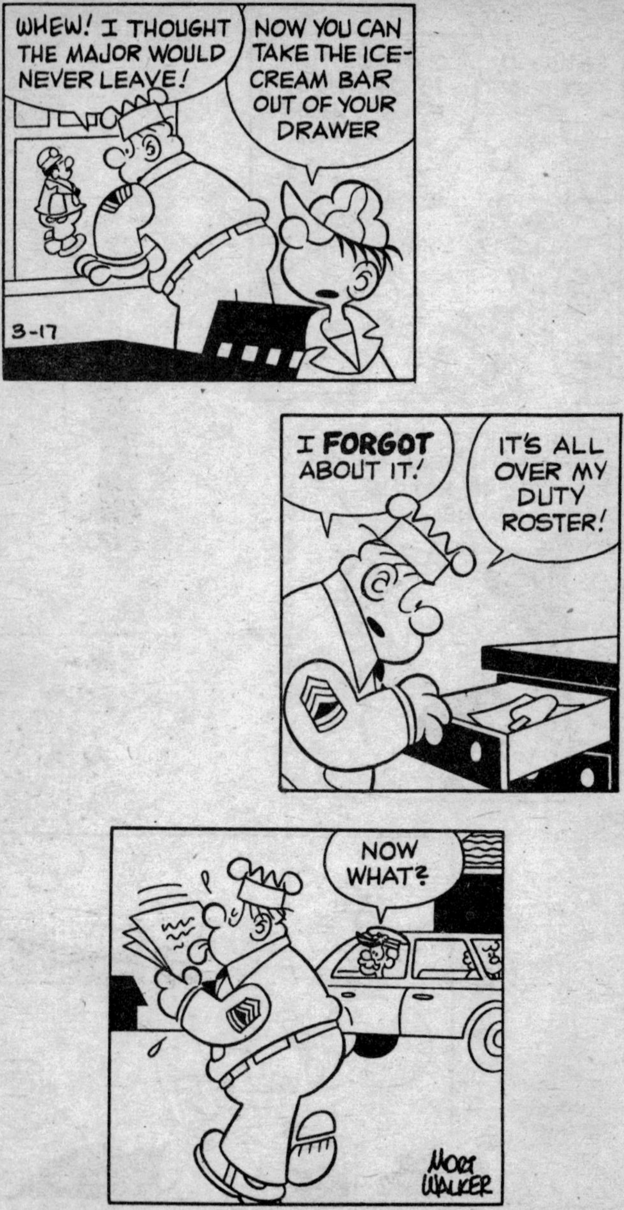
WHEW! I THOUGHT THE MAJOR WOULD NEVER LEAVE!
NOW YOU CAN TAKE THE ICE-CREAM BAR OUT OF YOUR DRAWER
3-17
I FORGOT ABOUT IT!
IT'S ALL OVER MY DUTY ROSTER!
NOW WHAT?
MORT WALKER

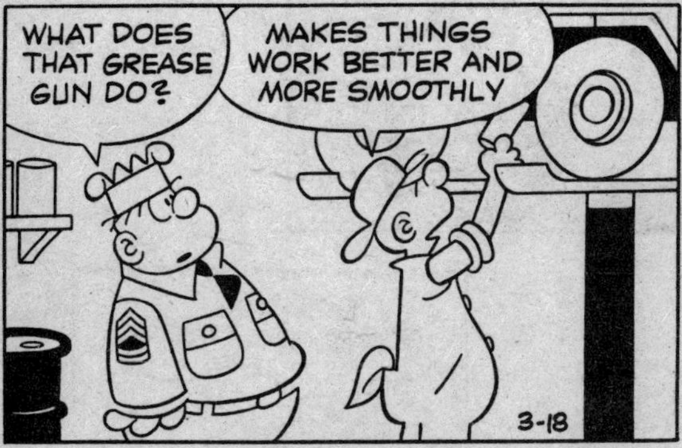
WHAT DOES THAT GREASE GUN DO?
MAKES THINGS WORK BETTER AND MORE SMOOTHLY
3-18

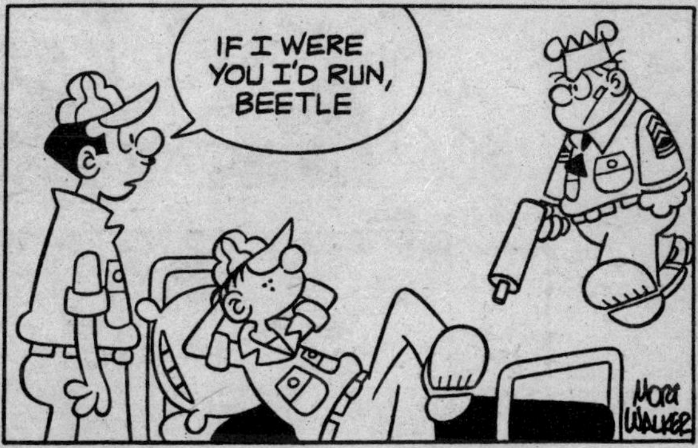
IF I WERE YOU I'D RUN, BEETLE
MORT WALKER

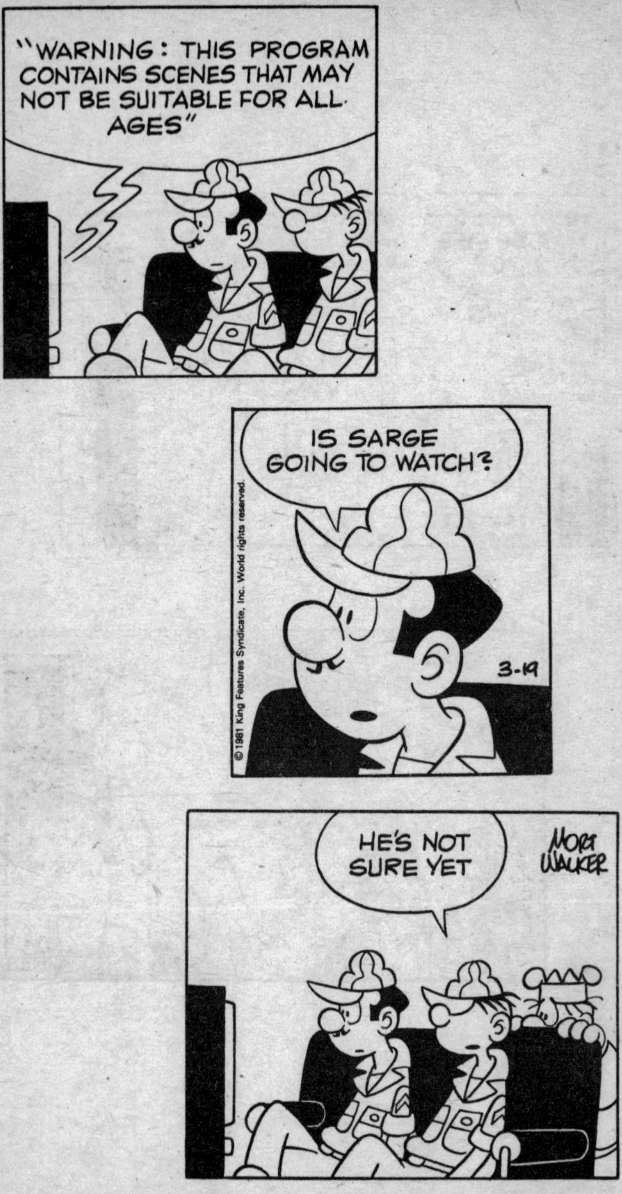
"WARNING: THIS PROGRAM CONTAINS SCENES THAT MAY NOT BE SUITABLE FOR ALL AGES"
IS SARGE GOING TO WATCH?
©1981 King Features Syndicate, Inc. World rights reserved.
3-19
HE'S NOT SURE YET
MORT WALKER

LOOK AT THAT BELLY. I WANT TO SEE YOU IN BETTER SHAPE, SARGE
3-20
I MEANT PERMANENTLY
MORT WALKER

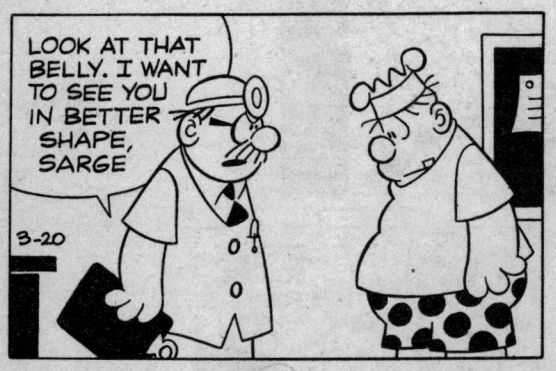

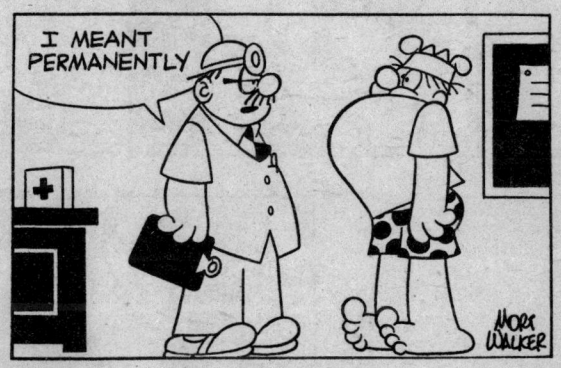

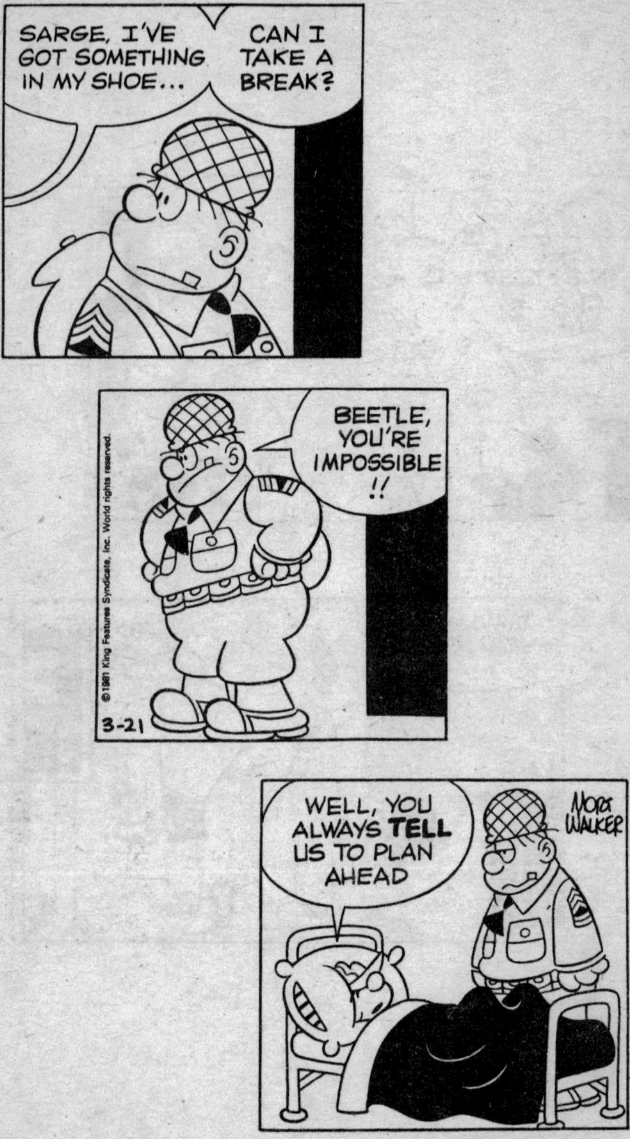
SARGE, I'VE GOT SOMETHING IN MY SHOE...
CAN I TAKE A BREAK?
BEETLE, YOU'RE IMPOSSIBLE !!
©1981 King Features Syndicate, Inc. World rights reserved.
3-21
WELL, YOU ALWAYS **TELL** US TO PLAN AHEAD
MORT WALKER

BEETLE, DIDN'T YOU KNOW I'D SEE YOU LOAFING RIGHT OUTSIDE MY WINDOW?!
YEAH
3-23
THEN WHY ARE YOU DOING IT?!
I'M TRYING TO QUALIFY FOR THE 1981 NATIONAL GUTS AWARD
MORT WALKER

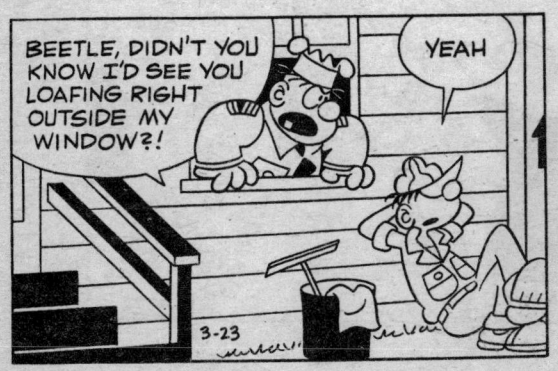

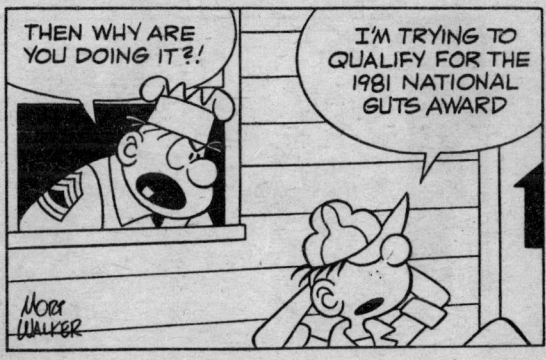

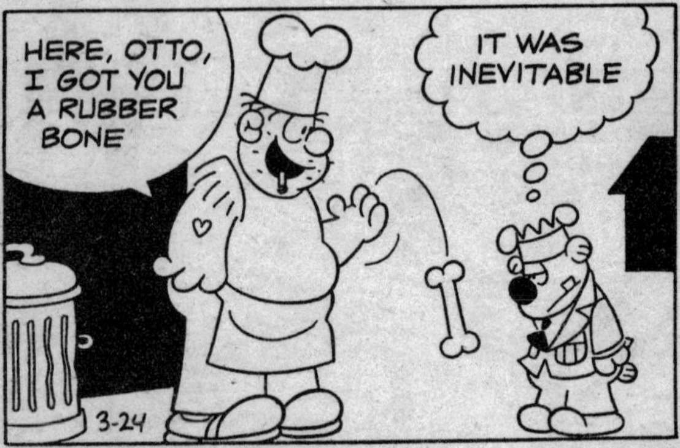
HERE, OTTO, I GOT YOU A RUBBER BONE
IT WAS INEVITABLE
3-24

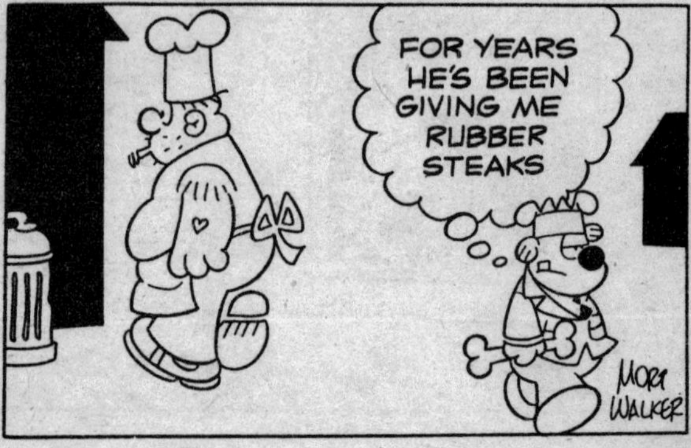
FOR YEARS HE'S BEEN GIVING ME RUBBER STEAKS
MORT WALKER

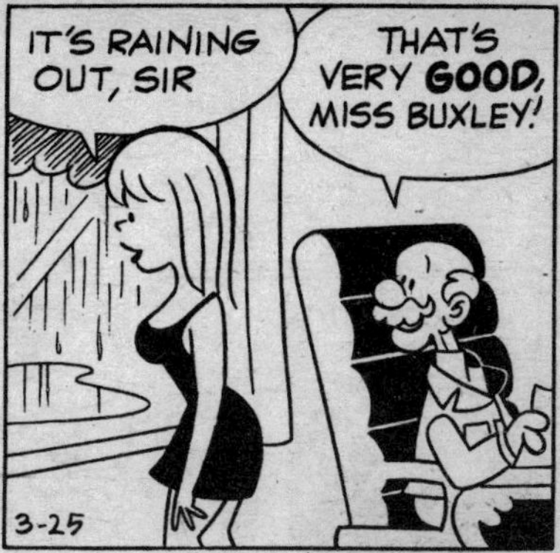
IT'S RAINING OUT, SIR
THAT'S VERY GOOD, MISS BUXLEY!
3-25

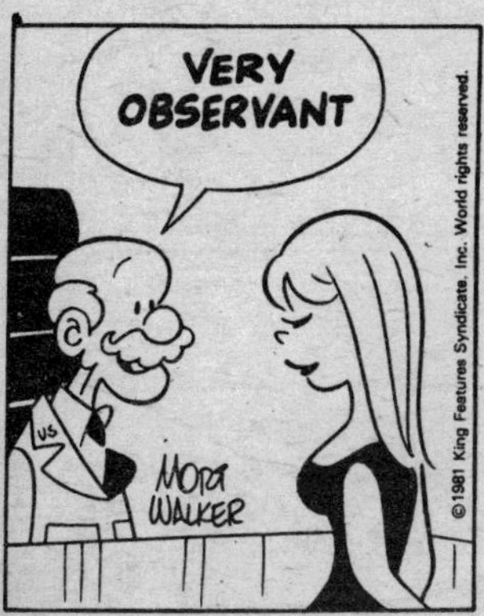
VERY OBSERVANT
MORT WALKER
© 1981 King Features Syndicate, Inc. World rights reserved.

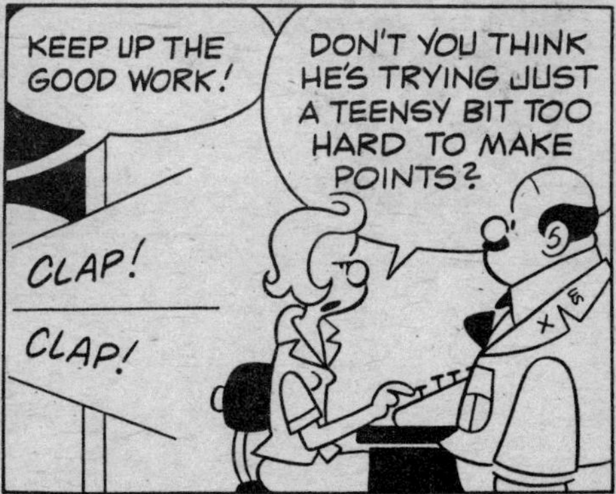
KEEP UP THE GOOD WORK!
CLAP!
CLAP!
DON'T YOU THINK HE'S TRYING JUST A TEENSY BIT TOO HARD TO MAKE POINTS?

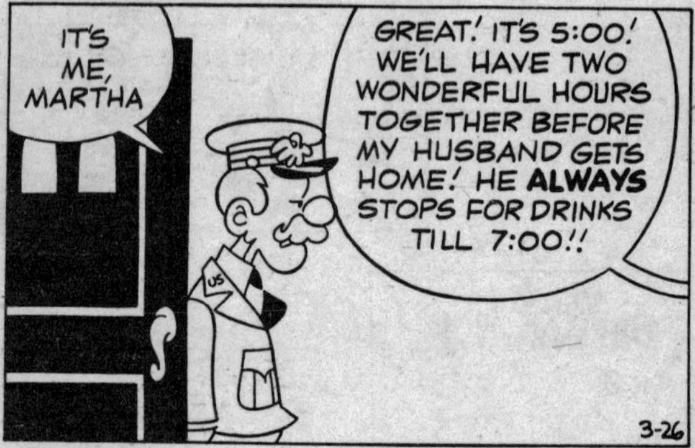
IT'S ME, MARTHA
GREAT! IT'S 5:00! WE'LL HAVE TWO WONDERFUL HOURS TOGETHER BEFORE MY HUSBAND GETS HOME! HE ALWAYS STOPS FOR DRINKS TILL 7:00!!
US
3-26

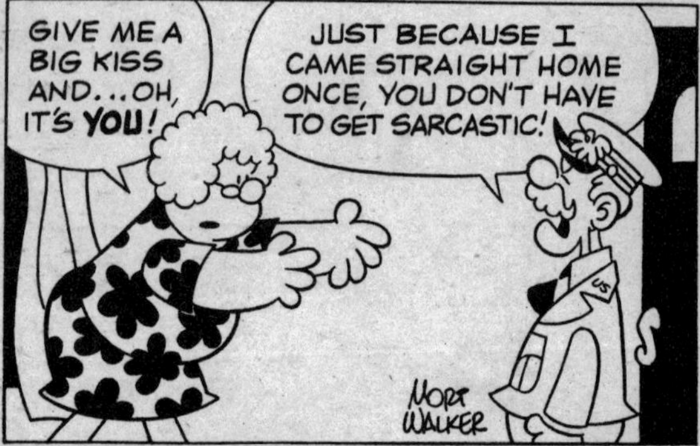
GIVE ME A BIG KISS AND...OH, IT'S YOU!
JUST BECAUSE I CAME STRAIGHT HOME ONCE, YOU DON'T HAVE TO GET SARCASTIC!
US
MORT WALKER

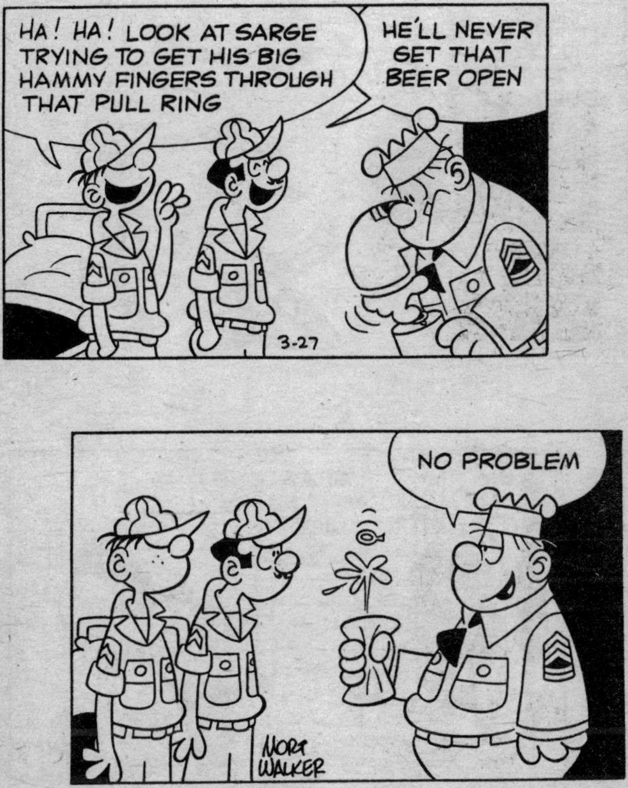
HA! HA! LOOK AT SARGE TRYING TO GET HIS BIG HAMMY FINGERS THROUGH THAT PULL RING
HE'LL NEVER GET THAT BEER OPEN
3-27
NO PROBLEM
MORT WALKER

WHAT'S THAT YOU'RE PUTTING IN YOUR GOLF BAG?
WIND-CHILL JUICE
3-28
JUST AS LONG AS IT ISN'T LIQUOR
MORT WALKER

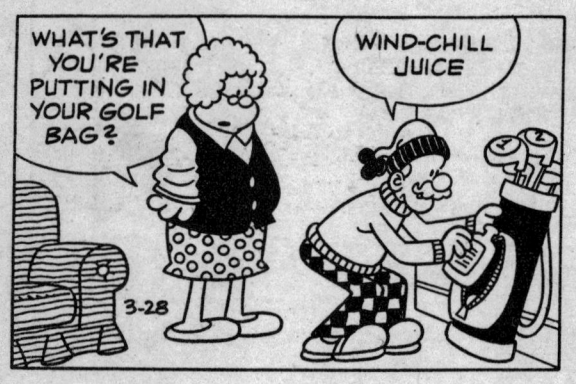

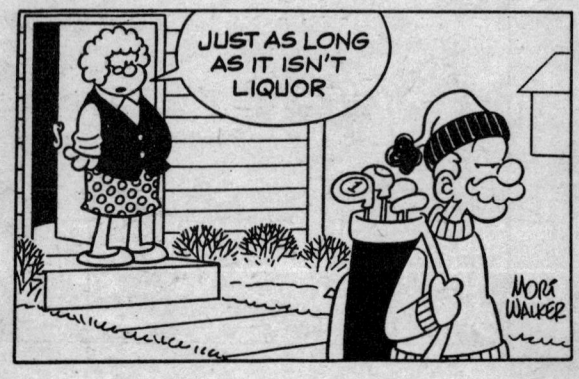

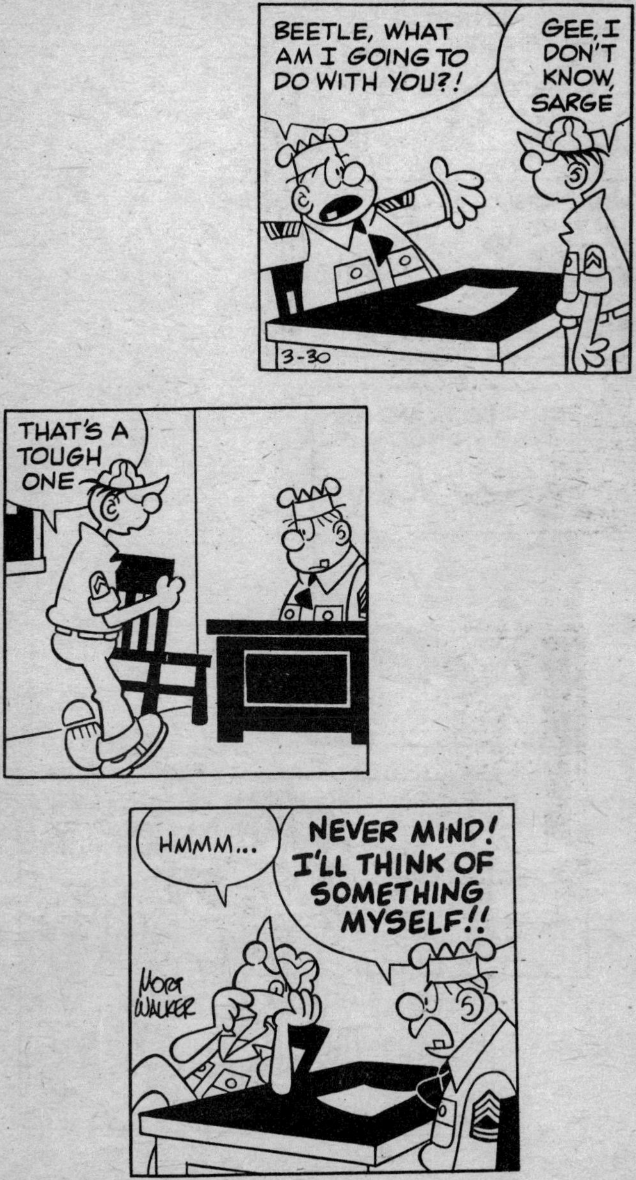
BEETLE, WHAT AM I GOING TO DO WITH YOU?!
GEE, I DON'T KNOW, SARGE
3-30
THAT'S A TOUGH ONE
HMMM...
NEVER MIND! I'LL THINK OF SOMETHING MYSELF!!
MORT WALKER

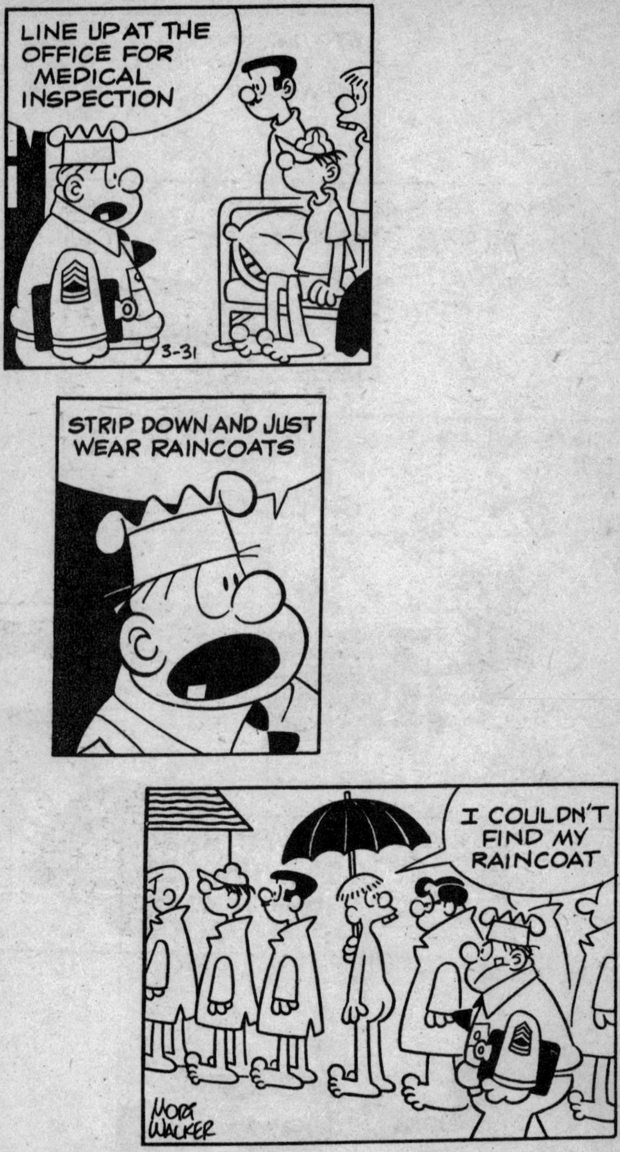
LINE UP AT THE OFFICE FOR MEDICAL INSPECTION
3-31
STRIP DOWN AND JUST WEAR RAINCOATS
I COULDN'T FIND MY RAINCOAT
MORT WALKER

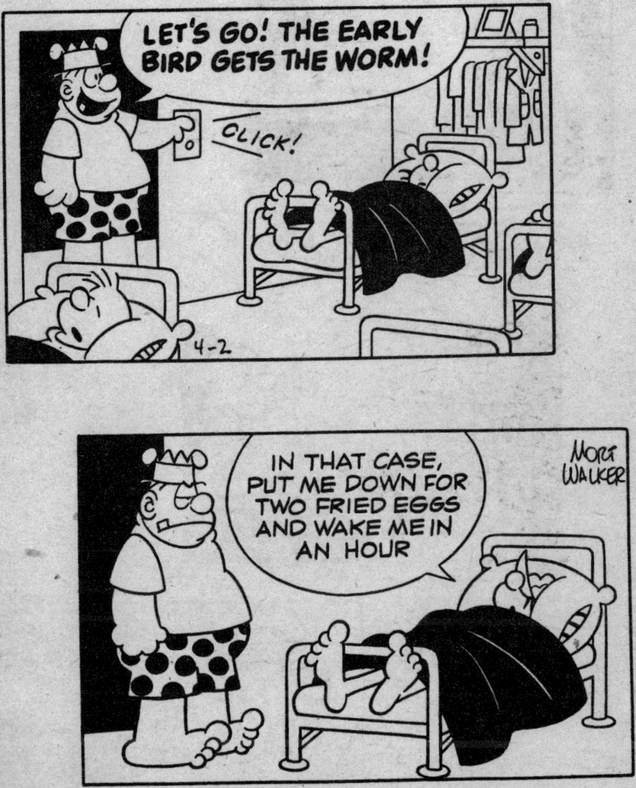
LET'S GO! THE EARLY BIRD GETS THE WORM!
CLICK!
4-2
IN THAT CASE, PUT ME DOWN FOR TWO FRIED EGGS AND WAKE ME IN AN HOUR
MORT WALKER

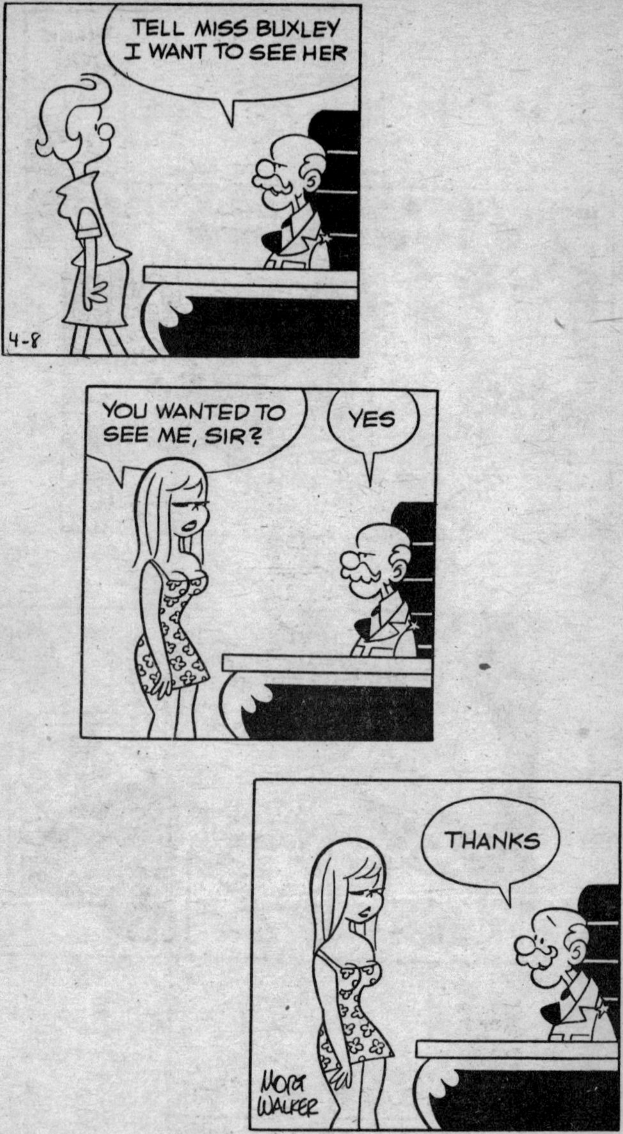
TELL MISS BUXLEY I WANT TO SEE HER
4-8
YOU WANTED TO SEE ME, SIR?
YES
THANKS
MORT WALKER

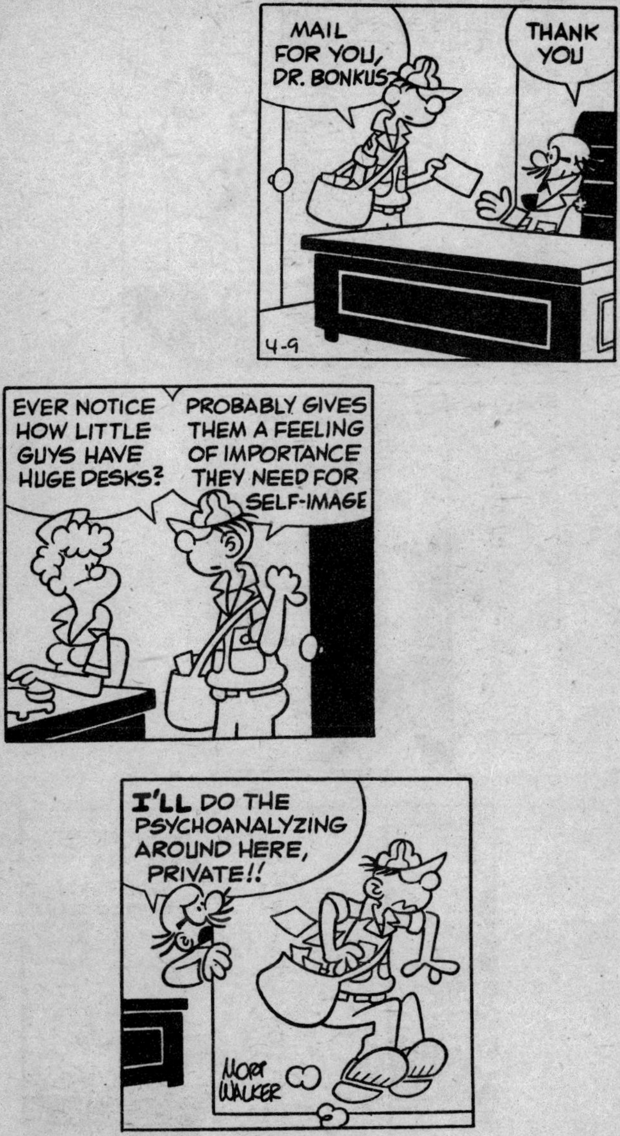
MAIL FOR YOU, DR. BONKUS?
THANK YOU
4-9
EVER NOTICE HOW LITTLE GUYS HAVE HUGE DESKS?
PROBABLY GIVES THEM A FEELING OF IMPORTANCE THEY NEED FOR SELF-IMAGE
I'LL DO THE PSYCHOANALYZING AROUND HERE, PRIVATE!!
MORT WALKER

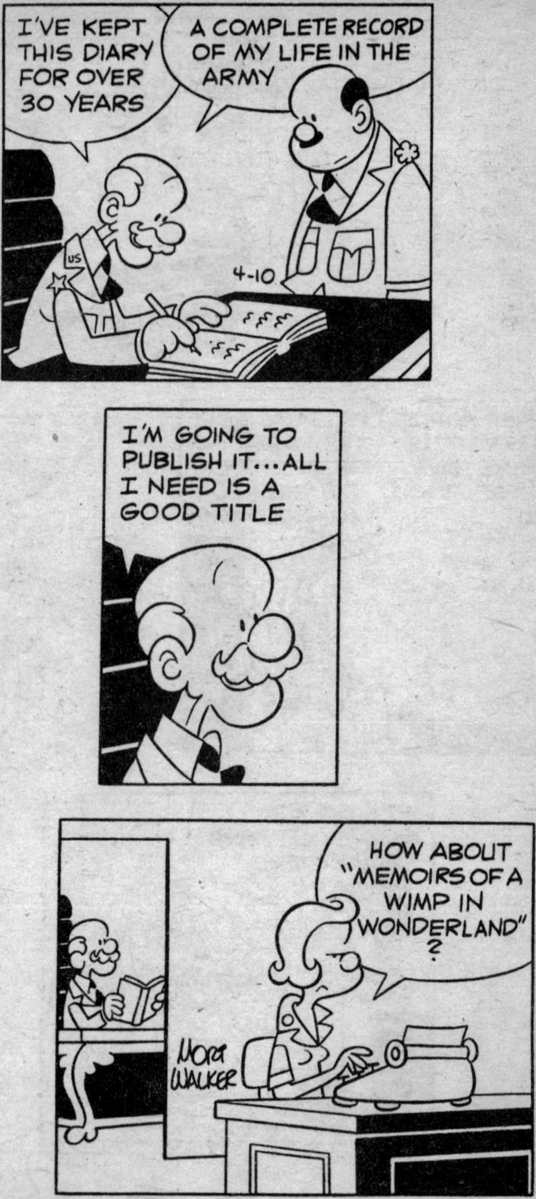
I'VE KEPT THIS DIARY FOR OVER 30 YEARS
A COMPLETE RECORD OF MY LIFE IN THE ARMY
4-10
I'M GOING TO PUBLISH IT...ALL I NEED IS A GOOD TITLE
HOW ABOUT "MEMOIRS OF A WIMP IN WONDERLAND"?
MORT WALKER

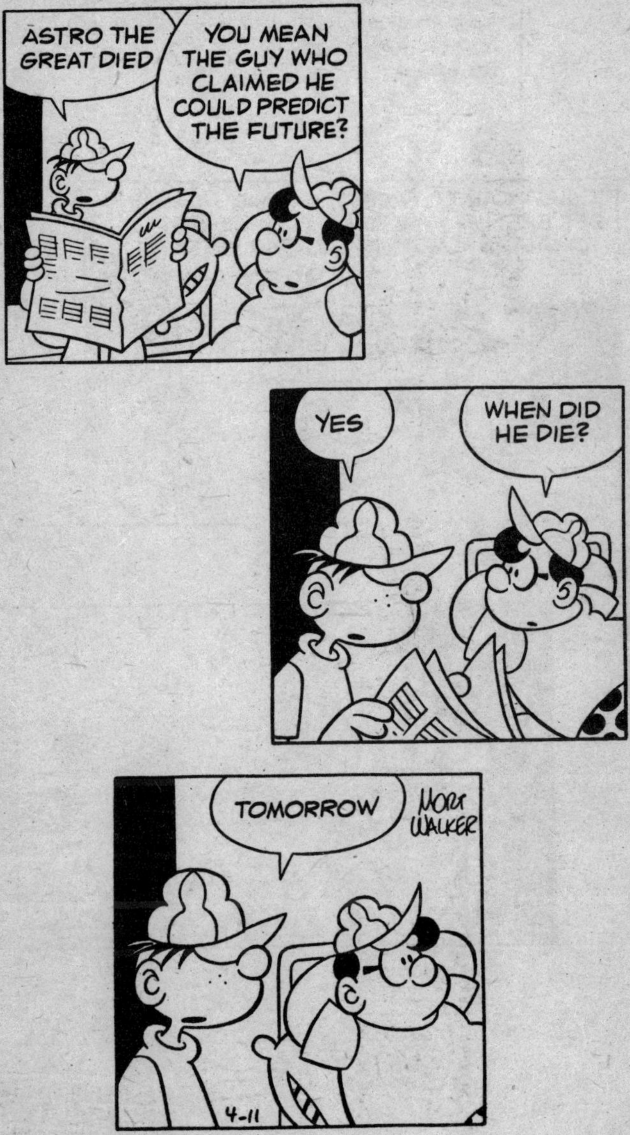
ASTRO THE GREAT DIED
YOU MEAN THE GUY WHO CLAIMED HE COULD PREDICT THE FUTURE?
YES
WHEN DID HE DIE?
TOMORROW
MORT WALKER
4-11

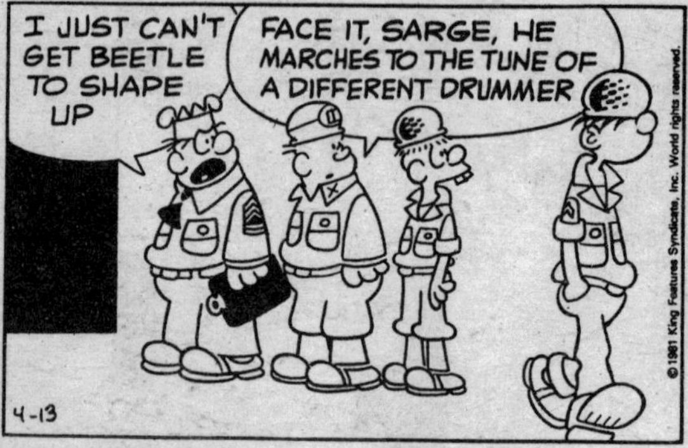
I JUST CAN'T GET BEETLE TO SHAPE UP
FACE IT, SARGE, HE MARCHES TO THE TUNE OF A DIFFERENT DRUMMER
4-13
© 1981 King Features Syndicate, Inc. World rights reserved.

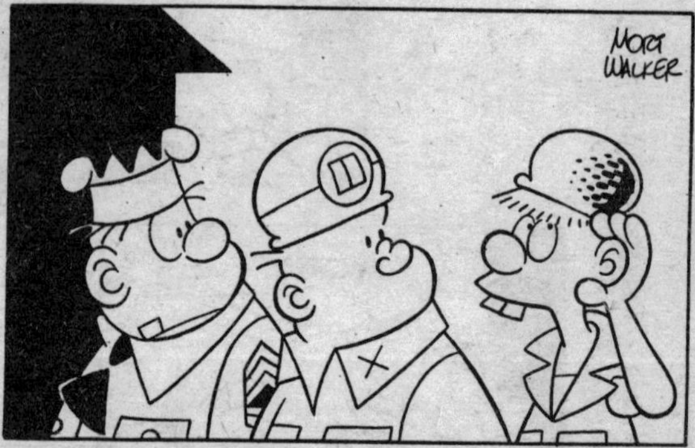
MORT WALKER

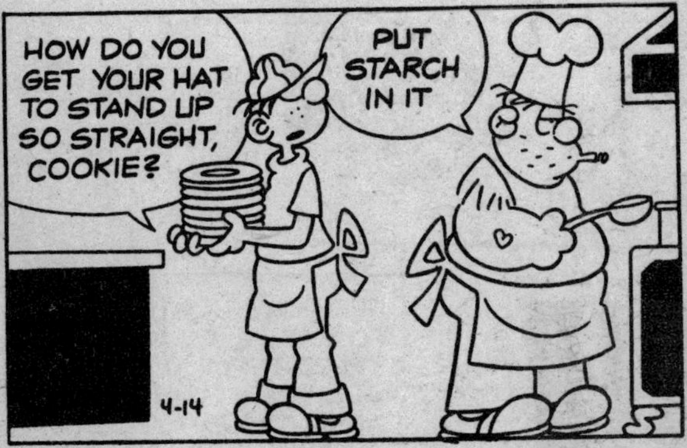
HOW DO YOU GET YOUR HAT TO STAND UP SO STRAIGHT, COOKIE?
PUT STARCH IN IT
4-14

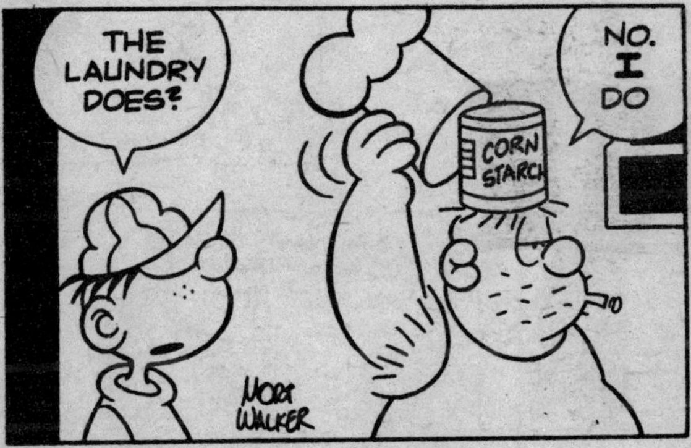
THE LAUNDRY DOES?
NO. I DO
CORN STARCH
MORT WALKER

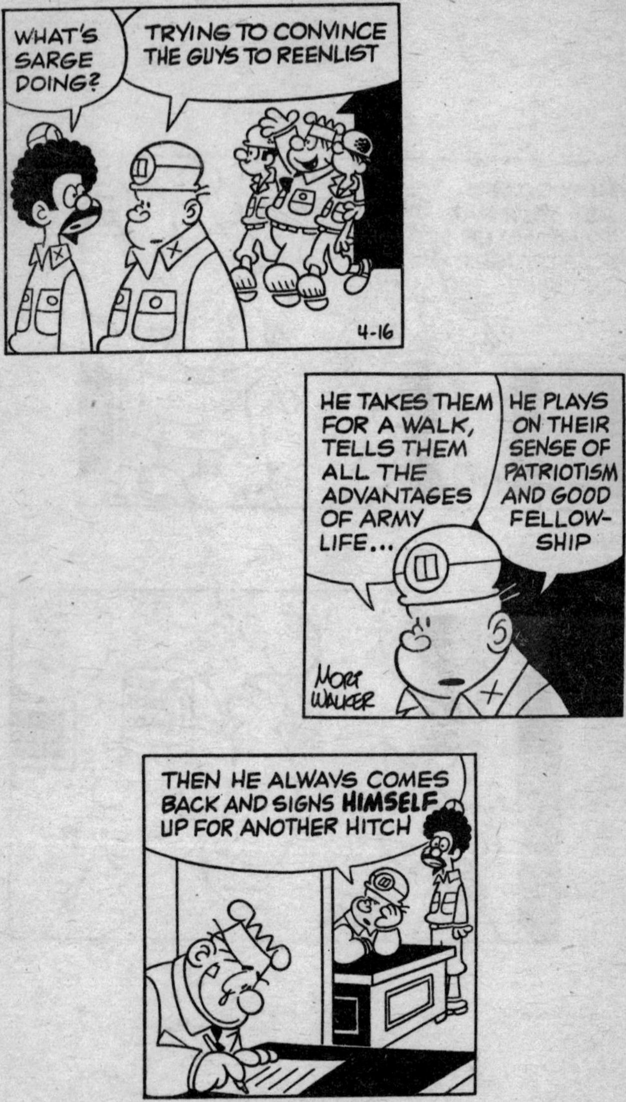
WHAT'S SARGE DOING?
TRYING TO CONVINCE THE GUYS TO REENLIST
4-16
HE TAKES THEM FOR A WALK, TELLS THEM ALL THE ADVANTAGES OF ARMY LIFE...
HE PLAYS ON THEIR SENSE OF PATRIOTISM AND GOOD FELLOW-SHIP
MORT WALKER
THEN HE ALWAYS COMES BACK AND SIGNS HIMSELF UP FOR ANOTHER HITCH